ISLAM
A
RAGING
STORM

ISLAM
A
RAGING
STORM

By
Dr. Shelton L. Smith

SWORD of the LORD
PUBLISHERS

Post Office Box 1099 • Murfreesboro, Tennessee 37133

Printed and Bound in the United States of America

Contents

1. Violent Terrorism Elicits Various Views............1

2. The Hate-Filled History of Islam 13

3. The False Faces of Islam............21

4. The Contrast of Christianity and Islam 43

5. Witnessing to Muslims and Winning Them to Christ 49

Additional Material for the Revised Edition

6. Persecution of Christians in Islamic Countries............57

7. Muslim Activities Around the World 85

8. Muslims in America............107

9. The Climate in the U.S. 121

Chapter One

Violent Terrorism Elicits Various Views

When the terrorist-commandeered airplanes began falling from the sky on September 11, the whole world was suddenly riveted to the television news. The events were surreal, so shocking as to stagger the most seasoned veterans among us.

By the time the second airplane hit the World Trade Center, we all knew it was a terrorist attack; we just didn't know who it was or why they would do such a thing. Within a matter of hours the answers to our pressing questions were coming into focus!

Somewhere in the world there were madmen—villainous, bloodthirsty psychotics—so motivated by hate and driven to evil that they would strike in such a murderous and cowardly fashion. It was unthinkable! Then as reality began to set in, we were made to realize it was true. Little by little, piece by piece, the unthinkable became the incomprehensible when it was known that the attacks were perpetrated by religious zealots, Islamic militants, Muslim extremists. In the name of a god and in the fervent exercise of their religion, they, with malice aforethought, commissioned their followers to perpetrate those heinous and horrendous acts!

What kind of religion could it be that would captivate so many to hate so deeply? In this book, I want to examine this and to provide some answers to the probing questions which have arisen from these events. In this first chapter we will take note of the opinions expressed and positions taken in the weeks following September 11, 2001, by various individuals, especially the religious spokesmen from various groups.

America's Official Response

All of us were thrilled when President George W. Bush faced the cameras and addressed the American people with such openness, such candor, such resolute determination and conviction!

Thankfully, he set in motion every resource at his command to bring the murderous lunatics to justice and to wipe out every known vestige of terrorism on the planet. As I write, the effort is moving forward successfully and with continued commitment to be victorious. We are fully supportive of the war effort. We pray for the president and for all of our military who are engaged in this conflict.

In an effort to send a message to the entire Islamic world, President Bush made clear, and I think rightly so, that America's call to arms was not a war against Islam but against terrorists. It is important that all of us understand that the goal of the American military campaign is to obliterate terrorism, not Islam. It was necessary for the president clearly to state that and to send that message lest millions of Islamic followers would react against us. We believe the president is correct to this point.

However, we do not believe he is correct when he says, "Islam is a religion of peace and love." It is our view that in this he has misjudged and misstated the situation. Again, we understand why, for purposes of politics and diplomacy, he made the statements; but we believe very firmly that the facts are indeed quite different. Every American and especially Christians need to be aware of Islam's true nature and its very real agenda! It is vitally important that we be alert to Islam's workings in our society. No longer is it some foreign news item that has no bearing upon us. It is now on our doorstep—banging on the front door trying to get in. We believe the facts will show that there is much reason to be concerned to the point of alarm and that we should be neither ignorant of it nor naive about it.

Some Evangelical Leaders Spoke Up and Struck Out

Jerry Falwell was one of the first Christian leaders to speak up. To a shocked and grieving nation it sounded like he

2

was saying that because of abortion and other moral decadence America had it coming and that September 11 was the judgment of God. His words were off-the-cuff, ill timed and did not resonate well. Apologetically he tried to clarify his views, but it was too little too late. Words spoken in haste are often difficult to explain. To his credit, he has recently said, "I was wrong. None of us can accurately say whether this was the judgment of God" (TV interview).

Pat Robertson initially agreed with Falwell but hastily retracted his complicity. Some of his efforts to explain himself appeared less than candid. He couched language too carefully, was red-faced and rambling, trying to undo the damage he had done! (TV interviews).

Billy Graham, speaking on September 14 at the National Cathedral in Washington, D.C., said, "We come together today to affirm our conviction that God cares for us, whatever our ethnic, religious or political background may be" (*World*, 12/1/01). In his typical ecumenical style, he was trying to legitimize the face of every religious philosophy present for the occasion. It was a political-type statement, reaching to all quarters but failing miserably to address the emerging realities of the crisis.

On the other hand, Franklin Graham, Billy's son and his recently appointed successor, spoke clearly and forthrightly: "We're not attacking Islam, but Islam has attacked us. The God of Islam is not the same God. He's not the son of God of the Christian or Judeo-Christian faith. It's a different God, and I believe it is a very evil and wicked religion" (*World*, 12/1/01).

Amazingly, I found myself actually nodding in agreement with something that came from the Graham headquarters, but it was not to last. Within a few hours he too was watering down his comments and explaining himself away:

> Now Franklin is in trouble with political friends for comments made recently, calling the entire Islamic religion "wicked, violent and not of the same God," *NBC News* said. "There is fallout from such remarks...."

Following the NBC report, Graham said...: "It is not my primary calling to analyze Islam or any other religions, though I recognize that all religions have differences. In the past, I have expressed my concerns about the teachings of Islam regarding the treatment of women and the killing of non-Muslims, or 'infidels.'" He said that he did not intend to comment further (CNS, 11/19/01).

One of the prototype "contemporary" churches in Chicago went so far as to invite a Muslim cleric to speak from their platform shortly after September 11:

Following the September 11 attacks,...Bill Hybels, of the Willow Creek Community Church, was increasingly bothered by reports of hate crimes and misinformation about Islam. "I was so concerned by the gap between Muslims and Christians that I thought Willow could do something about that," he said, according to the *Chicago Tribune*.

That "something" was to have his church invite a local Muslim leader, Fisal Hammouda, to talk about Islam to a total of 17,000 churchgoers, spread out over four services. "There are some Christians spreading half-truths that the Koran encourages violence," Hybels told his congregation....

...Hammouda was questioned by Hybels onstage in the 4,500-person auditorium. Hybels asked, "It appears that Osama bin Laden directed the attack [on September 11]...What do you think?" Hammouda said at first he thought "it couldn't be a Muslim," explaining that the Koran does not allow violence against innocent people...."We believe in Jesus, more than you do, in fact," Hammouda said, drawing laughter when Hybels, smiling, ventured to disagree.

"Muslims consider Jesus and other biblical figures to be Islamic prophets—though not as important as Muhammad—and we have all the prophets from the Bible," Hammouda said.

Other Evangelicals Spoke Decisively and Without Waffling

Paul Weyrich, president of the Free Congress Foundation, called for the U.S. Postal Service's year-old "Eid Greetings" stamp to be rescinded and "overprinted with the image of the twin towers," because "America's most notable experience with Islam was the attacks on September 11" (*USA Today*, 11/20/01).

Southern Baptist spokesman R. Albert Mohler, Jr. (president of Southern Baptist Theological Seminary), says,

Extremists may kill innocent people in the name of Allah,

but that is not the ultimate danger of the Islamic faith. The biggest danger is that Islam presents a false gospel, a false god and a false salvation (*Baptist Press*).

Syndicated columnist and Christian newsman Cal Thomas said,

President Bush invited 50 ambassadors from Muslim countries to the White House Monday for a traditional Iftar meal, breaking the sunrise-to-sunset daily fast of Ramadan. The ambassadors knelt and touched their foreheads to the floor of the East Reception Room. It's unlikely they were praying Lee Greenwood's lyrics for "God Bless the USA."...

Similar efforts to pacify those who hate us were tried by a group of Christian clergy more than 20 years ago. They visited Iran, hoping to persuade the Ayatollah Khomeini to release American hostages. Instead of the Christians praying in their traditional way, they prayed in the Islamic fashion with their foreheads on the ground.

The imagery of submission to Islam could not have been missed in the Muslim world [*The* (Nashville) *Tennessean,* 11/21/01].

WCC Defends Islam

World Council of Churches [WCC] head Dr. Konrad Raiser sent a letter in November greeting the worldwide Muslim community at the beginning of Ramadan. He evoked the spiritual bonds uniting Christians and Muslims that "need to be rediscovered in the aftermath of the September 11 tragedies." He said: "As Christians, we reject the tendency, not uncommon in many Western countries, to perceive Muslims as a threat and to portray Islam in negative terms while projecting a positive self-image." He called for "intensification of dialogue between religions and cultures." A copy of the letter to Muslim leaders was also sent to WCC member churches and to other ecumenical bodies. In an enclosed note, Raiser asked them to "seek the most appropriate ways" to engage with Muslim partners in acts of spiritual fellowship and prayer for peace and justice. He expressed solidarity with the Muslim community and of "our commitment to the spirit of dialogue and mutual trust." He wrote: "All acts which destroy life, whether through terrorism or in war, are contrary to the will of God. The recent tragic events [reveal] the vulnerability of all nations and the fragility of the international order. A world in which more and more people and nations are consigned to extreme poverty while others accumulate great wealth is inherently unstable. The tendency to impose one's will, even by force—which is [seen] in the policies of powerful nations, provokes resentment among the weaker ones....Here the dialogue between Muslims and Christians, to which the World Council of Churches remains strongly committed, finds its authentic meaning" (11/16/01 WCC e-mail via *Calvary Contender*).

The WCC, as well as its American counterpart, the National Council of Churches (NCC), is a notoriously left-of-center bastion of liberalism on everything.

They have for many years shown themselves friendly to communism, socialism and a wide array of other less-than-desirable elements. They have typically spoken in friendly terms of almost anyone and anything except fundamental, conservative Christians.

There is nothing that we know of about which we could commend the WCC. They are in all things an apostate outfit.

We have shown here their positioning of themselves on the Islam matter because this is the fodder they will feed to the 337 denominations in their membership. Consequently, many of the clergy in those denominations will parrot these same lines when they stand before their congregations on Sunday. It is just one more reason why folks who have continued their worship with WCC- or NCC-affiliated churches should bail out immediately!

For the sake of your influence and for the well-being of your family, you should take leave of these ungodly associations and cast your lot with Bible-believing Christians.

Pope Calls for Peace Summit

Pope John Paul II....has called...[a] meeting at Assisi of the world's religious leaders for January 24 to pray for peace and to work to improve relations between Christians and Muslims, which deteriorated after the September 11 terrorist attack on the U.S. He has told Jews, Muslims and other non-Christians: "We believe in the same God" (7/15/88 *Calvary Contender*). The pope also urged Catholics to hold a fast for peace (11/23/01 *Religion Today* via *Calvary Contender*, 1/1/02).

Understandably, we do not expect to get a Bible perspective from the pope, but his expressed opinion makes clear the perspective that is going to be taught to as many as a billion Catholics worldwide. We have many Catholics who read the SWORD, and I want to make strong the case to each one of them: The pope is wrong! He is not only NOT infallible, but he is positively, absolutely in error (on this and a lot of other things too).

As we will later document in this book, the god of Islam is not "the same God" that we know and serve.

We cannot make peace with a religion like Islam that is dedicated to the destruction of everything which does not "submit" to it. To do so is to forfeit everything we hold dear, including our freedom.

However, many of these religious leaders, like the pope and the WCC, are blinded to the truth by their own agenda. Our appeal to people everywhere is: Don't be fooled about Islam by the ecumenical rhetoric of these errant leaders!

Fundamental Leaders of North America Speak With Conviction and Courage

In interviews with the Sword of the Lord, several leading fundamental pastors and evangelists spoke clearly and strongly. Their voices reflect a bedrock of scriptural convictions. Courageously yet compassionately, to a man, they stood up and spoke the truth.

Dr. Raymond Barber, author of numerous Sword-published books, longtime pastor in Fort Worth, Texas and now a popular Bible conference speaker, said:

> We are opposed to Islam, not because we are intolerant of another person's religion, but because of the precepts set forth in Islam and in the Koran—that is, to kill, to abolish and to destroy anything that does not embrace Islam. They brand anyone not Islamic as "infidel." We would have to oppose Islam because it is anti-Bible and anti-Christianity.

Dr. Clarence Sexton, pastor of the large, growing Temple Baptist Church in Knoxville, Tennessee and president of Crown College, told the Sword:

> Our Christian Faith is founded on the Bible and operates from the liberty of the soul. We are free in Christ Jesus. Islam

7

is a religion of bondage and fear. It operates from the edicts of man. I think that's the difference.

Dr. Norris E. Belcher, Jr., pastor of the Church of the Open Door in Westminster, Maryland, the largest fundamental church in the Northeast, told us:

Islam means "to submit." A true Muslim submits to the five pillars of Islam. The first pillar is the confession: "There is no god but Allah, and Muhammad is his prophet." The second is praying five times daily, facing Mecca. The third is the giving of alms. The fourth is the observance of Ramadan. The fifth is the pilgrimage. There is no repentance, no sacrifice for sin, no new birth and no Saviour! It is therefore impossible to correlate Islam with Christianity! The god of the Koran is not the God of the Bible! Islam is a false religion based on a false god.

Dr. Greg Baker, pastor of FaithWay Baptist Church and president of FaithWay Baptist College in Ajax, Ontario, Canada, says:

The exclusive claims of Jesus Christ and the Bible place Islam into the category of a false religion. The Bible is the Christian's final authority, and Jehovah God is the only God (Deut. 4:35), and Jesus Christ is the only Saviour (Acts 4:12).

Dr. Mickey Carter, pastor of the Landmark Baptist Church (one of Florida's largest independent Baptist churches) and president of Landmark Baptist College in Haines City, Florida, and a respected voice among Bible-believing Christians, said:

Allah is not the Jehovah of the Bible but was worshiped as the moon god by the Quraysh tribe into which Muhammad was born. This is where the crescent moon on top of the mosque comes from. It is a religion of the sword, not love. As an example of this, we just had a young Muslim couple and their baby killed (when they returned to their homeland) because they converted to Christ. America needs to awake to this dangerous false religion.

Dr. Bob Kelley, pastor of one of South Carolina's largest churches, the Grace Baptist Church of West Columbia, citing a basic contrast between Christianity and Islam, said:

Islam has no Gospel. Our Saviour is alive from the dead.... Muhammad is dead. Period!

Pastor Lonnie Mattingly, the longtime pastor of the Shawnee Baptist Church in Louisville, Kentucky; founder and president of Shawnee Baptist College; a compassionate soul winner and a recognized leader in independent Baptist circles, told the Sword:

In contrast to the practice of Islamic nations, Bible-believing Christians make becoming a Christian a free choice of individual conscience, and there is no state penalty for a wrong choice. Although Bible Christianity teaches that Jesus Christ is the only way to Heaven, it does not fear other ideologies. Conversion to Bible Christianity is by the Word of God and the power of the Holy Spirit, not by fear and force.

Dr. R. B. Ouellette, pastor of the largest Baptist church in Michigan, the First Baptist Church of Bridgeport, and one of the nation's most sought after preachers, spoke to the heart of the conflict when he said:

The religion of Islam seeks to control by public coercion. The Koran in Surah 9:29 says, "Fight those who believe not in Allah...nor acknowledge the religion of the truth [Islam]...." Christianity seeks to convert by personal conviction. The followers of Islam loathe their enemies and want to destroy them. Christians love their enemies and want to deliver them. Most significantly, the religion of Islam follows a dead prophet; Christians serve a risen Saviour.

Dr. Fred Schindler, pastor of the Landmark Baptist Church in Downingtown, Pennsylvania, the founder and president of Northeast Baptist College, a seasoned veteran in fundamental circles, identified a crucial element in this crisis when he noted that the Muslim "holy book" is not the same as the Christians' Holy Bible! He said:

Muslims believe the Koran is the word of Allah, revealed to the prophet Muhammad. Christians believe the Bible is the Word of God given by the Holy Spirit about our Saviour, Jesus Christ, who died for us, was buried, rose from the dead and is alive. The writings of this one man do not begin to compare with the God-breathed writings of the Bible.

Sam Davison, pastor of the large, thriving Southwest Baptist Church in Oklahoma City, Oklahoma; president of Heartland Baptist Bible College and one of the nation's strongest pulpiteers, reflecting on the track record of the past, said:

History declares that a nation shaped by the influence of authentic Christianity becomes the most inviting place in the world. On the other hand, there is no Statue of Liberty inviting the weary masses in the harbor or at the border of any Islamic nation.

Dr. Don Sisk, a missionary statesman, the executive director of Baptist International Missions, Inc., who has, by reason of his travels all over the world, had opportunity to observe firsthand the Muslim culture, told us:

> Islam, like all false religions, centers around what the followers do for Allah. Biblical Christianity centers around what God has done for us. "They shall call his name Emmanuel...God with us" (Matt. 1:23). He is with us (this "us" includes every person in the world) to show us who He is; to comfort us in every trial; to suffer, bleed and die for us; to be raised for our justification; to ascend to Heaven to be our Intercessor and to come one day to take us to His home where we will be together for eternity. Islam knows nothing of this kind of a personal Saviour.

Dr. George Riddell, the longtime pastor of the Open Bible Baptist Church in Williamstown, New Jersey, said in a recent interview with the Sword of the Lord:

> The strength of biblical Christianity is the living hope that we have in Christ (I Pet. 1:3). When contrasted with a people who follow Islam, which has no living hope whatsoever, we have a living hope that is in the work of Christ which was accomplished at Calvary (I Pet. 2:24). Our living hope is based upon His work at Calvary and upon His resurrection as well. We are serving a RISEN Lord!

The testimonies of these men of God need to be heard. Thankfully, we do have good men, seasoned men, men with the anointing of God on their lives, men who are committed to a scriptural agenda—not some social, philosophic or secular one. With frankness and with fervency, they are speaking the truth as men of God should. We need them to be visible and to be vocal. The survival of our nation may depend upon it.

Across our nation thousands of good, Bible-believing pastors stood up in the weeks following the attack and addressed the issues of war, violence and murder. As shepherds they sought to minister comfort to a frightened and grief-stricken nation who needed to hear the consolations of God from these men of God.

Most of us, preachers included, were only slightly acquainted with Islam prior to September 11, but in the wake of the violence there have been many questions about it.

Australian Baptist Editor, a Clear Voice

Paul B. Hunter, editor of the *Biblical Fundamentalist* in Brendale, Queensland, Australia—a good man, our friend and a stalwart Christian advocate—says:

> Islamic leaders in the West, and even our own government, are now declaring that Islam is a peaceful religion which does not condone terrorism and stands for freedom.

> It's obvious that those who are making these claims know little or nothing about the religion of Islam.

> If what these people are saying is true, why are Muslims responsible for most of the terrorism in the world today?

> Muhammad was the one who declared war against the entire world in the seventh century, and since then *jihad* (holy war) has been waged by Islamic warriors to spread their religion of violence and hatred....

> Since September 11, we are repeatedly told by well-intentioned government officials that we must be careful not to blame Islam for what a few fanatics have done; but terrorists act in direct obedience to Muhammad, the Koran, Allah and Islam. While nominal Muslims reject the idea, all Islamic scholars agree that it is the religious duty of every Muslim to use violence whenever possible to spread Islam until it has taken over the world....

> America has been called "the Great Satan" by Muslim leaders around the world. Attacking America was a strike for Allah against his chief enemy. This kind of "suicide" has long been an honorable Islamic practice.

> It may be true that many Muslims are peace-loving and would protest that they oppose terrorism. However, they should ask themselves why they follow a religion founded upon violence which from its very inception has been spread with the sword....

> In the West, Islam presents a face of peace; but when it is strong enough, it will turn to war. ISLAM DOES NOT CHANGE! (*Biblical Fundamentalist,* Dec. 2001).

* * *

In this book we will offer what we believe to be sufficient evidence that Islam is a false religion offering a false god with a false hope which fosters and promotes hate, violence and other wickedly atrocious things. We will show how Islam has made its mark on the world not by persuasion but by coercion—indeed, ruthless force, persecution and murder.

Christians, we believe, have a responsibility to stand up and sound forth the truth. While we are tolerant of other people's right to variant points of view, we expect their tolerance in return when we argue the cause of truth and error, right and wrong, light and darkness.

We will try to give the information about Islam that we believe Christian people need to know, we will raise the biblical issues that are pertinent, and we will offer some practical advice on what we should do and how we should do it. We will address the following:

(1) the history of Islam;

(2) why so many Muslims hate Christians;

(3) the Islamic agenda;

(4) the teachings of Islam;

(5) Bible truths that expose Islam;

(6) how to witness to Muslims;

(7) how Christians and America can survive Islam.

Chapter Two

The Hate-filled History of Islam

In the aftermath of the terrorist attacks on America (September 11, 2001), it became obvious almost immediately that the perpetrators were Middle Eastern militants with a fanatical devotion to Islam. Until then, Islam, for most Americans, was little more than "something religious" and "something foreign." All of that changed on September 11 when disciples of that foreign religion struck our homeland with powerful force and genocidal impact. Suddenly all of us became aware of Islam and the need to know what it is about!

What Is Islam?

Islam is first and foremost a religion. It is indeed a religion whose followers are known as Muslims or Moslems, founded by an illiterate, self-professed prophet named Muhammad, who lived from A.D. 570 to 632.

Islam began with the mystic visions of a nondescript camel driver named Ubu'l-Kassim (who became known as Muhammad). For six months he had been in solitary meditation in a cave at the foot of Mount Hira near Mecca. Had he not married a widow named Khadijah, fifteen years his senior, he might have spent his life on caravan journeys. Khadijah's wealth gave Ubu'l-Kassim the time he needed for ascetic reflection.

Muhammad was born in A.D. 570 in Mecca. He was yet a baby when his father died, and his mother passed away when he was six. Abu-Talib, an uncle, raised the young lad and took him on lengthy trips to Egypt and throughout the Near East. During these travels Muhammad engaged in lively conversations with Jews and Christians. From these encounters he learned the theological concepts that were later to influence his teachings.

...He was afflicted by a strange disorder that caused him to foam at the mouth and fall into unconscious trances.... Muhammad himself questioned whether the seizures were divine or devilish, but his wife encouraged him to ignore any such considerations....

To raise funds for his spiritual quest, Muhammad sanctioned plundering expeditions that raided caravans. Even during his native land's traditional month of peace, his followers mercilessly attacked innocent citizens. During this time when Muhammad ruled as a king and prophet, he forged the Islamic concept of the *jihad* ("exertion"), the "holy war" which advocates military ventures in God's name (Bob Larson, *Larson's Book of Cults,* Wheaton, Ill.: Tyndale House, 1983, pp. 104–106).

As a result of his numerous visits to the Hira cave where Muhammad claimed to have had visions of the angel Gabriel, he recited in summary what he had experienced. These recitations became the basis for what is now known as the Koran (Qur'an, meaning "recitation"). The Koran is not the only "holy book" of Islam, but it is the main one and the best-known one.

Although very familiar with Christianity and Judaism, Muhammad rejected them both. It is unclear whether he began to form his own theological perspective as a result of the cave visions or whether the cave visions are merely a mysterious cloak he invented to give credibility to his already developing ideology. Whichever it was, it represents the embryonic stage of what is now known as Islam.

The message of Muhammad did not resonate with the pagan cultures of his day. For twelve years (A.D. 610–622) he labored in relative obscurity and with only minimal success in convincing a following of people.

In A.D. 622 he supposedly was warned in a vision of a significant danger to himself, so he fled from Mecca to a refuge of safety 250 miles away in Yathrib, now known as the city of Medina. This journey is known in Muslim circles as "the flight." It was a turning point in Muhammad's efforts and is generally considered the real beginning of the Muslim era. The Muslim calendar dates the year of the flight to Medina as year one.

When Muhammad died without an anointed successor or without so much as a game plan for one, there was a time of struggle and infighting for control of the movement. Abu Bakr, one of Muhammad's longtime cohorts and an avid disciple, won the contest of leadership and was named the successor.

Shortly thereafter, the Muslim presence and influence began escalating. The one hundred years after the death of Muhammad saw the military muscle of the Muslims sweep into Palestine, Egypt and Syria, as well as what is now Iran and Iraq, plus North Africa and into Europe. These military excursions successfully imposed Islamic rule and offered no tolerance at all for anything non-Muslim.

In a most revealing and defining analysis, J. M. Roberts, author of *The History of Europe* (Allen Lane, 1996), says, "Islam from the start was a religion of conquest." That modus operandi has not changed. It is still the mentality which permeates the Muslim world.

> Filled with religious zeal, Muslim armies spread the message of Islam to India, across North Africa and into Spain. Had it not been for the Battle of Tours in A.D. 732, all Europe might have succumbed to the message of the Koran. A capital was established in Baghdad, and the *caliph* who ruled from there was the most powerful man on earth and headed a regime spanning three continents.
>
> The Islamic empire was to last for a thousand years (Larson, p. 106).

Some of that same military totalitarianism continued to be the means of the spread of Islam during the Dark Ages and beyond. Indeed, as we are now learning, the iron fist of Islam holds sway in dozens of countries today. Where their presence is sufficient to seize control, they are even now intolerant of others—vicious in their dealings to the point of torture and murders.

The tour of places where Islam dominates does not pose a pretty picture. It is the ugly face of tyranny, repression, violence, slavery and a thousand other archaically wicked "Stone Age" practices. Where in the world is Islam elevating the course of a nation and the lifestyle of its people? Where indeed is a place in which Islam is not ensnaring its adherents with poverty and stifling their freedom with its harsh and unmerciful despotism?

Is Islam a Religion of Peace?

Since September 11, 2001, we have been told over and over that the attacks against America do not represent the heart and core of Islam. The politicians have said it. Many of the clergy are also saying it. A number of religious ecumenical memorial services have been very careful to have Islamic presence on their platforms in an effort to legitimize the religion of Islam. It is our firm opinion that it is all a smoke screen and we should not be deceived by these naive and foolish attempts to make Islam look acceptable.

An excellent synopsis of the true nature of Islam is noted in a recent editorial by *Foundation* magazine editor Dennis Costella:

> Despite what we are hearing from politicians and religious leaders, Islam is not a religion of peace and tolerance. The very word *Islam* means "submission." We should be thankful that most Muslims here in the United States are people who desire peace in the world and who respectfully tolerate other religions. They do not take their "holy book" as literally as do Muslims in other areas of the world, and they are not defined as "fundamentalists" because they do not strictly obey what their religion teaches them. While most Muslim people in the Western world may be peaceful and tolerant, the religion of Islam itself is neither peaceful nor tolerant. Throughout the Middle East, the Muslim religion/culture is carried out to its natural end in nations such as Afghanistan, Pakistan, Libya, Yemen, Saudi Arabia and other countries. In these nations, no distinction exists between "mosque and state," and those who convert to a religion other than Islam are often punished or killed. Religious liberty is expressly forbidden. Proselytizers are not allowed. Women are enslaved. Infidels (those who reject Islam) are enemies of the religion and the state. *Jihad* (holy war) against the infidels is the natural outcome of this religion. Their "holy book" allows for this and actually encourages it.

In an interview aired on an Arab TV station and published by the Associated Press, Osama bin Laden, the man who on September 11 became the world's most wanted criminal, said:

> A target, if made available to Muslims by the grace of God, is every American man. He is an enemy of ours whether he fights us directly or merely pays his taxes....

Every Muslim, the minute he can start differentiating, carries hate towards Americans, Jews and Christians. This is part of our ideology. Ever since I can recall I felt at war with the Americans and had feelings of animosity and hate towards them (*The Christian News,* 10/15/01).

When we read such vitriolic, hostile words, we are shocked, and we ask ourselves, "What is his problem? What is behind all this?" The answer is very clear: The problem is, he is a Muslim, and it is Islam that is behind it all.

The simplicity and directness of the Koran has left no room for compromise. Its history, fables, regulations and threatening description of Hell compel believers into single-minded devotion. Jews are damned by Allah, and Christians are told that faith in Christ as God incarnate is "blasphemy....whoever joins other gods with God—God will forbid him the Garden, and the Fire will be his abode." (The doctrine of *shirk* forbids associating anyone or anything with God's divinity) (Larson, p. 106).

With an ideological foundation such as this, the Muslim world is a powder keg waiting for a match to light its fuse. It is a highly explosive ingredient in today's world. When these Islamic ideologues fan the flames of fanaticism religiously, governmentally, educationally, scientifically, economically, politically and militarily, it composes a gathering storm cloud of a greatly powerful and explosive force.

Does this mean that every Muslim is a soldier in the Islamic *jihad,* only awaiting the opportunity to strike? No, it doesn't mean that at all. Still, the fact is now well established that there are millions of Muslims who are militant adherents to their religion, enraged fanatics who are willing to do anything, including dying, to force Islam upon the non-Islamic world.

For some years now the threat of Islam has increased, as in one nation after another the militants have gained a presence of strength. Even where they do not physically dominate, they have often generated sufficient fear to intimidate and thus achieve their desired goals.

Presently there are at least forty-nine nations where Islam has established itself strongly enough that the rest of the world identifies each of those countries as an Islamic state. Some of those states are governed by somewhat more moderate factions, but in almost every case, the militant fanatics are steadily gaining in their strength and pose an ever increasing danger of taking full control.

True Islam is a religion of war and terrorization. That is the legacy of Muhammad. True Islam makes no distinctions between military and civilian; all are enemies of Allah if they are not Muslim at least in name....Regardless of what we are told, Islam is an anti-Christian religion. The best elements of it are willing to live in peace with all; the worst elements—those that most closely resemble the Islam of Muhammad—are determined to eradicate all others (*The BDM Letter,* Fall 2001).

The Different Attitudes Produced by Islam and Christianity

There's not a place in the world where Muslims are oppressed or persecuted by Christians. If indeed such a situation were to develop, even in some fringe area or with some lunatic group, the rest of us who are Christians would cry aloud against it and would exert our energies to get it stopped.

Oddly, it seems that the Muslim world has been strangely void of voices crying out against the September 11 attacks!

Christianity is not a faith of coercion and conquest. It is furthered by preaching and persuasion. Sure, we try to proselytize Muslims, but it is an effort born of compassion and caring, of love and personal freedom. No one is ever forced or in any way coerced to become a Christian.

In countries where Christians dominate or where their influence is pervasive, Muslims are permitted to come and go in the free exercise of their religion. Christians would not tolerate a situation where Muslims are harmed or restricted from their religious practices. Yet in almost all the Muslim-dominated countries, Christianity is illegal, its practice prohibited, and its adherents punished if caught.

Muslim-controlled countries suppress freedom of religion, freedom of the press, freedom to vote, freedom of speech, freedom of dissent—in fact, freedom in almost every sense; whereas, in countries where Christians have majority presence, freedom is cherished, promoted and defended for everyone, including Muslims.

While Islam forbids suicide, there is exception made for these fanatical "martyrs" who will give their lives in the process of snuffing out the lives of as many infidels (non-Muslims) as possible. Promises of paradise, virgin women and the like are the carrot sticks of enticement for this foolish and wicked effort. Christians are committed to the sanctity of human life as a gift from God and would not permit or promote anything which would bring harm to even one innocent life.

These practices noted above stand in stark contrast to one another. In our further analysis of Islam, we will have a section of their beliefs which we will differentiate from those of Christianity. Islam and Christianity are vastly different.

It is the difference between day and night, darkness and light.

As we get better informed about the whole Islamic scene, it is important that we learn to articulate the truth and give voice to our faithful witness to Muslims, as we do to anyone else.

Chapter Three

The False Faces of Islam

In the two previous chapters considering the religion of Islam, we have (1) reviewed the opinions of the media, our political leaders and a number of leading spokesmen in Christian circles and (2) taken a brief but factual look at the history of Islam, as well as (3) certain contrasts between Islam and Christianity.

Now we want to look closely at the actual substance of Islam, its teaching and its doctrines.

In his last major address to the nation of Israel, Moses made clear the choices before them and prophesied boldly of the impact their choices would have upon the future.

"See, I have set before thee this day life and good, and death and evil."—Deut. 30:15.

Now here we are in the twenty-first century confronted by Islam, and the choices we make will indeed have a real bearing upon us and upon succeeding generations. When the Bible tells us about God, the true God, and describes the conditions He produces in the human experience and in the earthly arena, it doesn't sound like Islam even in the least.

"This then is the message which we have heard of him, and declare unto you, that God is light, and in him is no darkness at all.

"If we say that we have fellowship with him, and walk in darkness, we lie, and do not the truth."—I John 1:5,6.

The presence of God and the mandates of His Word produce light and love, not hate and heartache. From Him come life and liberty, not death and destruction.

"Again, a new commandment I write unto you, which thing is true in him and in you: because the darkness is past, and the true light now shineth.

"He that saith he is in the light, and hateth his brother, is in darkness even until now.

"He that loveth his brother abideth in the light, and there is none occasion of stumbling in him.

"But he that hateth his brother is in darkness, and walketh in darkness, and knoweth not whither he goeth, because that darkness hath blinded his eyes."—I John 2:8–11.

When the devils of darkness rear their ugly heads, it is important for us to be perceptive, discerning, sufficiently equipped with truth and possessing godly wisdom lest we are engulfed in the blight of their darkness.

"Hereby know we the spirit of truth, and the spirit of error."— I John 4:6.

Truth is not error, and error is not truth. Truth is vital; error, vicious! Truth is reliable, the sustenance of life, the bedrock of eternity, the very essence of our hope; while error is corrupt at its core, the companion of fools, a peddler of lethal poisons, the protagonist of devastations, the practitioner of death, stranding its victims in anxious foreboding with no hope of Heaven—helpless, fearful and soon to die.

Error promises much but delivers not at all.

"There is a way which seemeth right unto a man, but the end thereof are the ways of death."—Prov. 14:12.

We believe assuredly that Islam is a way of death and destruction, that it is false in its entirety and is in truth an expression of an antichrist.

"...and as ye have heard that antichrist shall come, even now are there many antichrists; whereby we know that it is the last time."— I John 2:18.

In these days a vigilance is required which will discern truth from error and which will recognize the presence of false prophets among us.

"Beloved, believe not every spirit, but try the spirits whether they are of God: because many false prophets are gone out into the world."—I John 4:1.

Of course, our critics will say that we are harsh and judgmental, intolerant and lacking understanding of the diverse nature of today's world.

We believe, however, that despite the naive accusations of our detractors, we have good and ample reasons, cause sufficient, to brand Islam as a blatantly false religion!

Islam's False God

Allah! Who is Allah? What is his history, his track record? Is Allah just another name for the God of creation? Is Allah the same as Jehovah?

The Muslims' motto, called the *Shahadah,* says, "There is one god; his name is Allah; and Muhammad is his prophet." Is that true? Are they right?

No! That is NOT true! They are NOT right. Still, the repetitious recitation of this statement is the creed of Islam. For Muslims, the repeating of the *Shahadah* several times a day is the confession that is the essential expression of what it means to be Muslim.

Islam is monotheistic—that is, they believe in one god, namely, Allah! Although they do give Jesus Christ place as a prophet, they reject outright and forcefully the idea that He is God. The Koran says that Jesus Himself regards any claim for His divinity to be blasphemous (Surah 6:101; 9:30; 19:88, 89, 91, 92). To the Muslim, the doctrine of the Trinity is a claim of polytheism. To suggest that someone else is on the same level as Allah meets with their firm resistance. They believe that Christians who attest the truth of the Trinity or who ascribe deity to Jesus are "infidels." The Christian's beliefs about Jesus are considered to be superstitious and pagan. To the Muslim, Jesus was a prophet, but entirely human, only a man and never God.

The God of Islam is a very capricious one, too far removed from people to be personally involved or concerned. Not only is he impersonal, but he also emphasizes judgment to the exclusion of love, and he motivates people by fear rather than by grace (Josh McDowell and Don Stewart, *Handbook of*

Today's Religions, San Bernardino, Calif.: Here's Life Publishers, Inc., 1983, p. 397).

The truth is, the Islamic Allah is a god borrowed from the mythology of the paganism which was prevalent in the Middle East in the time of Muhammad. In effect, Muhammad "created" Allah.

The Muslims claim that Allah in pre-Islamic times was the biblical God of the patriarchs, prophets and apostles. The issue here is thus one of *continuity.*

The Muslims' claim of continuity is essential to their attempt to convert Jews and Christians. If "Allah" is part of the flow of divine revelation in Scripture, then it is the next step in biblical religion....

The hard evidence demonstrates that the god Allah was a pagan deity. In fact, he was the moon god who was married to the sun goddess, and the stars were his daughters....

The Sumerians, in the first literate civilization, left thousands of clay tablets describing their religious beliefs....The ancient Sumerians worshiped a moon god who was called many different names....His symbol was the crescent moon....

The cult of the moon god was the most popular religion throughout ancient Mesopotamia....

In ancient Syria and Canna, the moon god Sin was usually represented by the moon in its crescent phase....

Everywhere in the ancient world the symbol of the crescent moon can be found on seal impressions, stoles, pottery, amulets, clay tablets, cylinders, weights, earrings, necklaces, wall murals and so on. In Tell-el-Obeid, a copper calf was found with a crescent moon on its forehead....Even bread was baked in the form of a crescent as an act of devotion to the moon god....

The archeological evidence demonstrates that the dominant religion of Arabia was the cult of the moon god. The Old Testament constantly rebuked the worship of the moon god (see, for example: Deut. 4:19; 17:3; II Kings 21:3,5; 23:5; Jer. 8:2; 19:13; Zeph. 1:5). When Israel fell into idolatry, it was usually to the cult of the moon god....

When the popularity of the moon god waned elsewhere, the Arabs remained true to their conviction that the moon god was the greatest of all gods. While they worshiped 360 gods at the Kabah in Mecca, the moon god was the chief deity.

Mecca was in fact built as a shrine for the moon god....

According to numerous inscriptions, while the name of the moon god was Sin, his title was *al-ilah,* "the deity," meaning that he was the chief or high god among the gods....

The moon god was called *al-ilah,* the god, which was shortened to Allah in pre-Islamic times. The pagan Arabs even used Allah in the names they gave to their children. For example, both Muhammad's father and uncle had Allah as part of their names. The fact that they were given such names by their parents proves that Allah was the title for the moon god even in Muhammad's day. Professor Coon says, "Similarly, under Muhammad's tutelage, the relatively anonymous *Ilah* became *Al-ilah,* the God, or Allah, the Supreme Being."...

Muhammad was raised in the religion of the moon god Allah. But he went one step further than his fellow pagan Arabs. While they believed that Allah (the moon god) was the *greatest* of all gods and the supreme deity in a pantheon of deities, Muhammad decided that Allah was not only the greatest god but the *only* god....

Is it any wonder then that the symbol of Islam is the crescent moon? that a crescent moon sits on top of their mosques and minarets? that a crescent moon is found on the flags of Islamic nations? that the Muslims fast during the month which begins and ends with the appearance of the crescent moon in the sky?

The pagan Arabs worshiped the moon god Allah by praying toward Mecca several times a day; making a pilgrimage to Mecca; running around the temple of the moon god called the Kabah; kissing the black stone; killing an animal in sacrifice to the moon god; throwing stones at the devil; fasting for the month that begins and ends with the crescent moon; giving alms to the poor; and so on.

The Muslim's claim that Allah is the God of the Bible and that Islam arose from the religion of the prophets and apostles is refuted by solid, overwhelming archeological evidence. Islam is nothing more than a revival of the ancient moon god cult. It has taken the symbols, the rites, the ceremonies and even the name of its god from the ancient pagan religion of the moon god. As such, it is sheer idolatry and must be rejected (Robert Morey, *The Islamic Invasion,* Las Vegas, Nev.: Christian Scholars Press, 1992, pp. 211–218).

Islam's False Prophet

Muhammad (A.D. 570–632) was the founder of Islam. Drawing his views and the concepts of Islam from a variety of other religions, including Judaism and Christianity, Muhammad blended select parts of each of them into his own religious philosophy and tradition. Prone to dreams and suffering from seizures, he at first thought himself possessed of a demonic spirit.

So perplexed was he by his doubts and struggles that Muhammad at one point had "grave doubts about his sanity" (ibid., p. 74). He was frightened and in such desperation that in a severely depressed state "he decided to commit suicide. However, on his way to the place where he was going to kill himself, he fell once again into a seizure" (ibid., p. 75). During the seizure "he experienced another vision in which he felt that he had been told not to kill himself but that he was truly called of God" (ibid., p. 75).

His wife, Khadijah, persuaded him to believe that his visions were from God. The messages in these visions were the thoughts of his mind which he felt he could distinguish from his own conscious cogitations.

An untutored man, unable to read or write, he rejected the various polytheistic religions of his day and espoused monotheism. Most believe that his acceptance of the view of one God came from his acquaintance with the influences of Judaism and Christianity to which he had been exposed.

> ...his character seems...to have been a strange mixture. He was a poet rather than a theologian; a master improviser rather than a systematic thinker. That he was in the main simple in his tastes...there can be no doubt...a shrewd judge and a born leader of men. He could, however, be cruel and vindictive to his enemies; he could stoop to assassination; and he was undeniably sensual (Sir Norman Anderson, Ed., *The World's Religions,* Grand Rapids, Mich.: Eerdmans, 1976, p. 52).

Violence and gentleness were at war within him. Sometimes he gives the appearance of living simultaneously in two worlds, at one and the same moment seeing the world about to be destroyed by the flames of God and in a state of divine peace; and he seems to hold these opposing views only at the cost of an overwhelming sense of strain (Robert Payne, *The Holy Sword,* New York: Collier Books, 1962, p. 84).

A strange man he was, with a mixture of ideas swirling inside of him. From his inner struggle came his "prophetic sayings" that form the substance of Islam. He lived a brief life, sixty-two years of it, and he died. The legacy he left is the Islamic religion. Its bloody history is shrouded with tyranny, death and destruction. Its presence and prominence have not and do not promote the betterment of the human race or the excellence of a society. One need only take a glance at the dozens of Islam-dominated countries. In most of them the standards of living are far behind the rest of the world. That is not without significance but is directly attributable to the prominence of Islam.

In the face of all that is known about Muhammad, there is no certification of his claim to be a prophet of God. He is instead a fraud, a false prophet, a preacher of ideas that do not represent the truth of Jehovah God.

Islam's False Book

The Koran, sometimes spelled Qur'an, is the so-called "holy book" of the Islamic religion. It is the authoritative scripture of Islam, the guide book that supersedes all others which may be viewed as scripture. It is comprised of 114 chapters, called *surahs,* all of which are ascribed to Muhammad, although some of them were written by his followers based on the oral traditions of what he had supposedly said.

> ...the Koran, containing prayers, rules of etiquette and calls to wage "holy war" (Larson, p. 111).

Muslims consider the Koran inspired and infallible. Much debate even among Muslim scholars has been centered upon whether the Koran is true or if certain portions of it are true.

The reliability of the claim to infallibility is called into serious question by the varied inconsistencies within the Koran. As an example, Dr. Robert A. Morey notes:

> In the Koran, we are told that Allah called Muhammad to be a prophet and an apostle. But as Dr. William Montgomery Watt observed, "Unfortunately, there are several alternative versions of these events."

In other words, the Koran gives us four conflicting

accounts of this original call to be a prophet. Either one of these four accounts is true and the others are false, or they are all false. But they all cannot be true.

In the Koran on four different occasions, Muhammad described his initial call to be a prophet and apostle.

We are first told in Surah 53:2–18 and Surah 81:19–24 that Allah personally appeared to Muhammad in the form of a man and that Muhammad saw and heard him.

This was later abandoned, and we are then told in Surah 16:102 and Surah 26:192–194 that Muhammad's call was issued by "the holy Spirit."

Since Muhammad does not really discuss who or what this "holy Spirit" was, this was later abandoned.

The third account of his original call is given in Surah 15:8 where we are told that "the angels" were the ones who came down to Muhammad and announced that Allah had called him to be a prophet.

Even this account was later amended in Surah 2:97 so that it was only the angel Gabriel who issued the call to Muhammad and handed down the Koran to him.

This last account of his original call was influenced by the fact that Gabriel had played a significant role in the birth both of Jesus and John the Baptist.

Some scholars believe that Muhammad assumed that it was only appropriate that the next great prophet in line, being himself, should also be issued the call by Gabriel.

This fourth and last account of his initial call is the one that most Muslims and non-Muslims have heard.

But we must point out that the same "incident" had four conflicting accounts given of it in the Koran (Robert Morey, *Islam Unveiled,* Sherman's Dale, Penn.: Scholars Press, 1991, pp. 72, 73).

Noted scholars—some Westerners, but others Islamic— shed some light on the discrepancies and the deficiencies of the so-called holy book of Islam:

The Scottish scholar Thomas Carlyle said, "It is as toilsome reading as I ever undertook, a wearisome, confused jumble, crude, incondite. Nothing but a sense of duty could carry any European through the Koran."

The German scholar Salomon Reinach stated, "From the literary point of view, the Koran has little merit. Declamation, repetition, puerility, a lack of logic and coherence strike the unprepared reader at every turn. It is humiliating to the human intellect to think that this mediocre literature has been the subject of innumerable commentaries and that millions of men are still wasting time in absorbing it."

Even the historian Edward Gibbon, who along with Reinach can hardly be accused of being Christians, described the Koran as, "An incoherent rhapsody of fable, and precept, and declamation, which sometimes crawls in the dust and sometimes is lost in the clouds."

McClintock and Strong's encyclopedia concludes that "The matter of the Koran is exceedingly incoherent and sententious, the book evidently being without any logical order of thought either as a whole or in its parts. This agrees with the desultory and incidental manner in which it is said to have been delivered."

Even the Muslim scholar Dashti laments the literary defects of the Koran: "Unfortunately the Koran was badly edited and its contents are very obtusely arranged. All students of the Koran wonder why the editors did not use the natural and logical method of ordering by date of revelation, as in 'Ali b. Taleb's lost copy of the text."

The standard Islamic reference work, *The Concise Encyclopedia of Islam,* refers to the "disjointed and irregular character" of the text of the Koran (ibid., pp. 104, 105).

The evidence against the legitimacy of the Koran is extensive. The claims made for it are fantasy and superstition.

We will later show that its contents do not commend its claims as a *"holy* book" at all. It is simply a garbled collection of the philosophy and pronouncements of a troubled soul named Muhammad.

Without substance to support its claims of inspiration and in consideration of its source and primary contributor, the self-styled prophet Muhammad, we reject it outright and label it as "a false book."

Islam's False Doctrines

In Islam there are five articles of faith and five pillars of faith. The five articles are the primary tenets or main doctrines of Islam. They are:

1. *God.* There is only one true God and his name is Allah.

Allah is all-knowing, all-powerful and the sovereign judge. Yet Allah is not a personal God, for he is so far above man in every way that he is not personally knowable....

Although Allah is said to be loving, this aspect of his nature is almost ignored, and his supreme attribute of justice is thought to overrule love.

The emphasis of the god of Islam is on judgment, not grace; on power, not mercy. He is the source of both good and evil, and his will is supreme.

2. *Angels.* The existence of angels is fundamental to Islamic teaching. Gabriel, the leading angel, appeared to Muhammad and was instrumental in delivering the revelations in the Koran to Muhammad....

All angels have different purposes, such as Gabriel...who is the messenger of inspiration. Each man or woman also has two recording angels—one who records his good deeds, the other, his bad deeds.

3. *Scripture.* There are four inspired books in the Islamic faith. They are the Torah of Moses, the Psalms (*Zabin*) of David, the Gospel of Jesus Christ (*Injil*) and the Koran. Muslims believe the former three books have been corrupted by Jews and Christians. Also, since the Koran is god's most recent and final word to man, it supersedes all the other works.

4. *Prophets.* In Islam God has spoken through numerous prophets down through the centuries. The six greatest are: Adam, Noah, Abraham, Moses, Jesus and Muhammad. Muhammad is the last and greatest of all Allah's messengers.

5. *Last Days.* The last day will be a time of resurrection and judgment. Those who follow and obey Allah and Muhammad will go to Islamic heaven, called Paradise, a place of pleasure. Those who oppose them will be tormented in hell....

Finally, there is a sixth article of faith which is considered by many to belong to the five doctrines....It is a central teaching of Islam—the belief in God's decrees of Kismet, the doctrine of fate. This is a very rigid view of predestination that states all good or evil proceeds from divine will (McDowell and Stewart, pp. 389, 390).

The five pillars of Islamic faith are the rules of conduct which are binding upon its adherents. They are:

(1) The reciting of the Shahadah. It is the motto of Islam,

and the Muslim is duty bound to express it daily: "There is one god; his name is Allah; and Muhammad is his prophet." It affirms the monotheistic nature of their god, Allah, and acknowledges the special status of their prophet, Muhammad.

(2) The daily prayers toward Mecca. Five times a day the Muslims kneel with their foreheads touching the ground while reciting ritualistic prayers.

(3) Almsgiving (zakat). Charity, once totally voluntary, is now established as an institutionalized tax in most Muslim countries, averaging about 2.5 percent annually.

(4) Fasting during the month of Ramadan. Between sunrise and sunset no eating or drinking is permitted. Since they are allowed to eat at night during Ramadan, it is not a true fast but one with a peculiar Muslim twist to it.

(5) The pilgrimage to Mecca (Hajj). Every Muslim must attempt to make this journey once in a lifetime as a deed of merit facilitating his salvation.

Once there, he walks seven times around the *kaaba* (cubical building housing a black stone). If the jostling crowd permits, he must also kiss the rock (probably a meteorite), which Muslims believe was carried to earth by Gabriel....Other holy sites in the area are visited, and a ritual sacrifice of goats, sheep or camels may be performed. Pilgrims may also throw stones at the sacred pillar to "stone Satan," reenacting the stones Ishmael heaved at the devil when the Evil One attempted to dissuade Abraham's son from submitting to his father's plans to offer him as a sacrifice. (The Koran says it was Ishmael, not Isaac, whom Abraham laid upon the altar of Mt. Moriah.)

Other beliefs and practices associated with Islam are: using a ninety-nine-bead rosary to recount the unmentionable names of Allah (the camel is the only creature said to know the 100th); holding mass-type services for the dead; forbidding statues and music in mosques; insisting on circumcision; veiling women's faces with the *purdah* and draping their bodies in the ankle-length *chador*; permitting polygamy; abstaining from drinking alcohol, eating pork and gambling; meeting for congregational worship at noon on Fridays; building *minarets* (towers from which to broadcast the call to prayer); abolishing a priesthood and having the *Imam* serve as spokesman for the faith; believing that Christ did not die

31

but was taken up to Heaven; teaching that Jesus will return in the last days to convert the entire world to Islam; and enforcing the "law of apostasy," whereby converts to other faiths (especially Christianity) may be imprisoned or lose their jobs and possibly their lives! (Larson, pp. 107,108).

Though briefly presented, the picture is clear as to the elements which constitute the fabric of Islamic faith. It is, we believe, filled with false teachings, false doctrines, a theological fraud, a scam to deceive the masses and unworthy of commendation or credential. Its theological foundations are riddled with false doctrine.

We urge upon our readers to discern truth from error with the realization that the difference is the essence of life and death, Heaven or Hell. Islam is a false religion which showed its head for the whole world to see on September 11, 2001. We must not allow the spinning of the facts by the media and others to distort the reality of it all.

Islam's False Teachers

Indeed the openly vocal advocates who stand up to articulate the Islamic message and espouse the Muslim cause are false teachers.

These false teachers of Islam are many. From Osama bin Laden to Yasser Arafat, from Saddam Hussein to Muammar Khaddafi, from Elijah Muhammad to Malcolm X to Wallace Fard to Muhammad Ali to Louis Farrakhan, there are a lot of them. They are here in America just as they are in various nations abroad. Some are military or political rulers; some are clerics; others are celebrities who have signed on with Islam and are now giving support by their influence; while still others are leaders of cultural revolution movements. Varied though they be, they are, one and all, false teachers of Islam. They are or have been on the scene in recent history hawking the tenets of Islam.

Following a false prophet, Muhammad, serving a false god, Allah, and taking instruction of the false doctrines of Islam from a false book, the Koran, these false teachers of Islam are duping multitudes of naive and often vulnerable people.

In "teachers" of Islam, we include not only the Muslim clerics but also all of those who, by their endorsement and encouragement, commend this false religion to the general public.

In less than two weeks after September 11, 2001, the Roman Catholic pope made a series of statements reported worldwide which reiterated the position he had taken often: Christians, Jews and Muslims worship the same God.

"From this place, I invite both Christians and Muslims to raise an intense prayer to the One Almighty God whose children we all are, that the supreme good of peace may reign in the world," Pope John Paul II told Christians and Muslims at an outdoor Mass in the Central Asian nation of Kazakstan on September 23. "Pope calls for Christians, Muslims to unite," an AP story in the September 24 *St. Louis Post-Dispatch* reported (*Christian News,* 10/1/01).

As incredible as it seems, this kind of ecumenical hocus-pocus is not confined to the Catholic hierarchy. Consider, if you will, the example of Robert Schuller, of California's Crystal Cathedral fame:

Audience of many faiths joins Schuller in mosque....

Ten years ago, Robert Schuller, veteran host of *Hour of Power,* the weekly televised church service, had never even met with a Muslim. Now the white-haired minister was basking in praises from two leading African-American Muslims in a Villa Park mosque.

"I've been watching...Schuller for approximately 30 years and have long been inspired by the *Hour of Power,*"...Louis Farrakhan told the crowd of Muslims, Christians, Jews and Sikhs at the interreligious event....

Wallace Deen Mohammed, the most prominent orthodox *imam* in the African-American community, recalled that his father, Nation of Islam founder Elijah Muhammad, warned him white people were devils.

Still, he said, "In my twenties, I watched the *Hour of Power,* [and] I didn't see any devil."...

Schuller has been touring to promote his new autobiography....But after the September 11 tragedy, Schuller said, he wanted to do more than peddle books.

"I wanted to have evenings of hope," he said.

So he spoke at an interfaith event where religious leaders all but outdid one another in their testimonies of positive change.

For decades, Schuller said, he was a proponent of the kind of proselytizing that pushed Muslims to become Christians. Then he realized that asking people to change their faith was "utterly ridiculous.".…

Farrakhan said that since a 1999 deathbed conversion he had moved from a nationalist Islam to a more universal Islam that saw the value of all faiths.

"I'm a Christian. I am a Muslim. I am a Jew. I am a Sikh. I am a Buddhist," he told the crowd.

Schuller's first interaction with a Muslim group came four years ago, when Mohammed invited him to give the opening sermon at the Muslim American Society's New Jersey convention. And in 1999, he was asked by the grand mufti of Syria to preach in Damascus.

"When I met the grand mufti…I sensed the presence of God," he wrote in his autobiography.

The two men, he said, focused on similarities.…

"In a world with crying children we have no time," he said.

"The purpose of religion is not to say, 'I have all the answers, and my job is to convert you.' That road leads to the Twin Towers. That attitude is an invitation to extremists," he said.

After September 11, he said, the emphasis should move from proselytizing "to just trying to help everybody who had hurts and hopes" (*Chicago Tribune,* 11/4/01).

Schuller's lack of discernment is no surprise to those of us who have observed him closely through the years. His espousing of that which the Scriptures call error has been a trademark of his ministry, so again we are not caught by surprise. His popular psychology, self-esteem gospel (his own term for it) and get-hold-of-your-bootstraps motivational jargon typically come garbed in Christian terminology. As a result, a lot of people have not understood what he really is; but honestly, if you look even casually at the *Chicago Tribune* report above, this represents a wholesale sellout of the Christian Faith! Shocking it is, even from someone like Schuller!

The diversity insanity that has such popularity in America these days seems to be the bandwagon of choice for a lot of people, including many "Christian" leaders.

While recognizing and acknowledging that we live in a

diverse culture, we also believe that it is vital that we "cry aloud" (Isa. 58:1) against those whose values and views are unsound. It is inherently heretical for so-called Christian or patriotic voices to seek to legitimize and give credibility and status to the face of an anti-Christ philosophy and religion.

Islam's False Faces

Salman Rushdie, author of *Satanic Verses,* who was for years forced into seclusion because of an Iranian death sentence imposed upon him because the book was not complimentary of Islam, recently said,

> "This isn't about Islam." The world's leaders have been repeating this mantra for weeks, partly in the virtuous hope of deterring reprisal attacks on innocent Muslims in the West, partly because if the United States is to maintain its coalition against terror it can't afford to suggest that Islam and terrorism are in any way related. The trouble with this necessary disclaimer is that it isn't true. If this isn't about Islam, why the worldwide Muslim demonstrations in support of Osama bin Laden and Al Qaeda?...

> ...[I]t would be absurd to deny that this self-exculpatory, paranoiac Islam is an ideology with widespread appeal (*Christian News,* 1/7/02).

The "love of peace" rhetoric is rendered weak and with little legitimacy as the heart and soul of Islam is now one step at a time being bared for the world to see.

I ask the Right Reverend Bullen Dolli, an Episcopal Bishop in Sudan, what he believes about the nature and intent of contemporary Islam. "It is a militant religion," he tells me and laughs at those who serve as its character witnesses.

Dolli was in Washington last week at the investigation of the Institute on Religion and Democracy. He attempted to warn Congress and anyone else who would listen of the dangers to his country and the United States posed by Islam, especially in its militant form.

"In Sudan," says Dolli, "the coercive instruments of the state use brutal force to ensure that no other religion but Islam is practiced" (Cal Thomas, *The Journal,* 10/27/01).

"But the American Muslims are different," comes the clatter of the spinmeisters! The relative quiet of American Muslims after September 11 may be partially explained by understanding where many of them really stand.

The *Washington Post's* Marc Fisher recently visited a Muslim school in [a] D.C. suburb. What he found ought to send chills up every American spine. An eighth-grader told Fisher: "If I had to choose sides, I'd stay with being Muslim. Being an American means nothing to me. I'm not even proud of telling my cousins in Pakistan that I'm American" (ibid.).

Why did not many thousands of them sound off, march in the streets, issue strong statements of condemnation of terrorism? Why have we not heard American Muslims strongly support our country? The reason seems obvious!

Why do they talk "love and peace" when the nations with Islamic rule are notoriously oppressive to women and children?

Why in the name of "love and peace" do the Islamic nations have such restrictive and oppressive laws toward Christians?

In 83% of nations where the majority of the population are Muslims, there is systematic government persecution of Christians. This persecution includes imposing the death penalty for sharing the Christian faith with a Muslim; national laws prohibiting conversion from Islam to Christianity; destruction of churches and murder or expulsion of Christian missionaries. Even in the few predominantly Muslim countries where the government does not openly participate in the persecution, it ignores and even encourages illegal persecution by Muslims against Christians (Tom Barrett, *Conservative Truth,* 12/16/01).

While the Muslim world and its advocates are posing as a civilized and legitimate presence in the world, the real character of Islam simply must not be ignored. Behind its public relations false face, there is an emerging recognition of its ugly and evil nature.

Karen Armstrong, author of a best-selling book about Islam, reports that the "vast majority of Muslims...are horrified by the atrocity of September 11." President George W. Bush says bin Laden represents a "fringe form of Islamic extremism...rejected by Muslim scholars and the vast majority of Muslim clerics."

Evidence from the Muslim world suggests otherwise. With the exception of one government-staged, anti-bin Laden demonstration in Pakistan and very few prominent Islamic scholars, hardly anyone publicly denounces him. The only Islamic scholar in Egypt who unreservedly condemns the September 11 suicide operations admits he is completely isolated. American officials are still waiting for Muslim politicians to speak up. "It'd be nice if some leaders came out and said that the idea the U.S. is targeting Islam is absurd," notes one U.S. diplomat.

They do not because the Muslim world is bursting with adulation for the Saudi militant. "Long live bin Laden," shouted 5,000 demonstrators in the southern Philippines. In Pakistan, bin Laden's face sells merchandise, and massive street rallies leave two persons dead. Ten thousand march in the capitals of Bangladesh and Indonesia. In northern Nigeria, bin Laden has (according to Reuters) "achieved iconic status," and his partisans set off religious riots leading to 200 deaths. Pro-bin Laden demonstrations took place even in Mecca, where overt political activism is unheard of.

Everywhere, the *Washington Post* reports, Muslims cheer bin Laden on "with almost a single voice." The Internet buzzes with odes to him as a man "of solid faith and power of will." A Saudi explains that "Osama is a very, very, very, very good Muslim." A Kenyan adds: "Every Muslim is Osama bin Laden." "Osama is not an individual, but a name of a holy war," reads a banner in Kashmir. In perhaps the most extravagant statement, one Pakistani declared that "bin Laden is Islam. He represents Islam." In France, Muslim youths chant bin Laden's name as they throw rocks at non-Muslims.

Palestinians are especially enamored. According to Hussam Khadir, a member of Yasser Arafat's Fatah Party, "bin Laden today is the most popular figure in the West Bank and Gaza, second only to Arafat." A 10-year-old girl announces that she loves him like a father. Nor is she alone. "Everybody loves Osama bin Laden at this time. He is the most righteous man in the whole world," declares a Palestinian woman. A Palestinian Authority policeman calls him "the greatest man in the world...our Messiah" even as he (reluctantly) disperses students who march in solidarity with the Saudi (Daniel Pipes, *The Journal*, 10/25/01).

Various polls have been done in the Islamic world. The numbers are revealing!

In the Palestinian Authority, a Bir Zeit poll found that 26

percent of Palestinians consider the September 11 attacks consistent with Islamic law. In Pakistan, Gallup found a nearly identical 24 percent reaching this conclusion (ibid.).

As appalling as it is, it appears that at least half of the people professing Islam are at least sympathetic to, if not altogether supportive of, Osama bin Laden, including his attack on America in September 2001.

The false face of Islam is a very real part of their story.

It has been said, "When in the minority they are meek like a lamb, when they are on an equal footing they are as cunning as a fox and as wily as a serpent, but when they are in the majority they become as bold as lions" (author unknown).

Islam's False Hope

You simply cannot start with a false god, a false prophet and a false book and produce a true picture of life and death, time and eternity. Bad eggs are not the ingredients of a good omelet! False ingredients can never constitute a true result.

Over the years the word *Islam* has come to mean to Muslims "submission." It is the essence of their religion. They must yield themselves in total submission to Allah.

The Koran has various passages which are contradictory to one another. On one hand there are statements which seem to be respectful of non-Islamic religions such as Judaism and Christianity.

However, a thorough examination of the Koran reveals that other passages are openly hostile and inflammatory to Christians and Jews. For example, just take note of these quotes directly from the Koran:

"The punishment of those who wage war against Allah and His Messenger, and strive with might and main for mischief through the land is: execution, or crucifixion, or the cutting off of hands and feet from opposite sides, or exile from the land: that is their disgrace in this world, and a heavy punishment is theirs in the Hereafter."—Surah 5:33.

"And fight them on until there is no more tumult or oppression, and there prevails justice and faith in Allah altogether and everywhere; but if they cease, verily Allah doth see all that they do."—Surah 8:39.

"O Prophet! rouse the Believers to the fight. If there are twenty amongst you, patient and persevering, they will vanquish two hundred: if a hundred, they will vanquish a thousand of the Unbelievers: for these are a people without understanding."—Vs. 65.

"So when the sacred months have passed away, then slay the idolaters wherever you find them, and take them captives and besiege them and lie in wait for them in every ambush, then if they repent and keep up prayer and pay the poor-rate, leave their way free to them; surely Allah is Forgiving, Merciful."—Surah 9:5.

Historically and currently where Islam has dominance there is a track record of murder, tyranny and persecution. Even the Islamic disciples are held in limited freedom and treated harshly and without due process. The hope of Islam for elevating the status of a society is a false hope.

In reference to eternity the greatest allure of Islam seems to be centered upon these suicide missions. Islam offers to its followers no real guarantee of Heaven except for the suicide bombers who kill unbelievers (non-Muslims) in the process. For them there is an assurance of paradise with a full complement of delights, including an ample supply of young virgins. What a sham!

So we assert that the hope of Islam—for both here and hereafter—is a false hope, a lie, an evil scheme of the Devil to deceive and to destroy.

"The thief cometh not, but for to steal, and to kill, and to destroy: I am come that they might have life, and that they might have it more abundantly."—John 10:10.

"Neither is there salvation in any other: for there is none other name under heaven given among men, whereby we must be saved."—Acts 4:12.

* * *

Since I presented this material on Islam in the SWORD OF THE LORD I have received numerous letters of support and encouragement. At the same time there have been other letters of angry reaction. I expected that, so I am not shocked by it. As a result, let me make some concluding observations:

(1) We are not peddlers of hate or warmongers. Yet what fools would we be if after the September 11 attacks we just sat idly by and waited for the next assault! Do not confuse the facts by accusing us of warmongering when we support the efforts of the American military to eradicate the perpetrators of the murderous evil of last September 11! Such mud may be thrown, but it will not stick because it is a phony charge.

We do NOT hate the Afghans, the Saudis, the Syrians or any of those who live in the Islamic countries! I repeat, we do NOT hate them, and we do NOT wish to harm them in any way. However, we will NOT be silent about their evil and deadly philosophy that garbs itself as the religion of Islam. Truth must be spoken; evil must be exposed! Since Islam is not the truth and since it is now known to be the custodian of evil, we must speak out! We do so NOT from a posture of hate but rather from the tower of truth and love and of a sound mind!

(2) We expect religious groups (even those with whom we disagree) to proclaim their message, to practice their faith and to persuade whomever they wish to do likewise; but what we do not expect and, in fact, find to be totally unacceptable and intolerable is persecution, coercion to convert, tyranny and violence to ensure compliance. Do not ask us to be silent about the perpetration of such evil practices! We must sound the alarm, and we will not even think of giving in to intimidation or threats.

(3) We must not be naive about Islam, its world view, its goals and its willingness to use violent methods to achieve its ends! What has been happening repeatedly in Israel is truly to be expected again and again in the US, Canada and the rest of the civilized world if we do not address it strongly. The hate that has been generated from inside the mosques all over the world is now spewing forth like the venom of a poisonous asp! The source is Islam! If the Islamic enthusiasts wish to reinvent their image in the world, then they too must stand up against the tyranny and violence. Otherwise, they may expect to be viewed as being in sympathy with the evil ones.

Islam is, we believe, a false religion. Seven areas are noted here. It has (1) a false god! It was founded by (2) a false prophet! It is based on (3) a false book! It perpetrates (4) false doctrines! Its advocates are (5) false teachers! It postures itself with (6) a false face! And it offers (7) a false hope to those who submit to it!

In the remainder of this book we will look at the contrast between the message of Islam and the message of Christianity. We will also offer ideas on just how to go about witnessing to and winning Muslims to Christ.

Chapter Four
The Contrast of Christianity and Islam

As this study has progressed, the image of Islam that has unfolded before us is not a pretty picture. For those of us who are Christians and for a lot of people who are not Christians but are nonetheless sane, thinking, reasonable people, the concepts of Islam are a bitter pill to swallow.

We cannot comprehend a god who sends his people on suicide missions designed to eliminate as many non-Islamic people as possible! We can't abide the frenzied expressions of hate being vocalized by millions of Islamic followers! We are baffled by a religion that rises forcefully and violently in nation after nation to coerce the population into submission to Islam! We are appalled by Islam's totalitarianism! We are aghast at the Islamic societal structure which preaches and practices the abusive treatment of women and children! We are shocked by the oppressive persecution practiced so unapologetically against Christians, Jews and other non-Islamic followers.

In the weeks following the terrorist attacks, the Islamic spokespeople in America were on the TV and radio talk shows desperately trying to give reassurances to all of us that they are nice people and that Islam is really a wonderful and peaceful religion. During several such appearances (where I was a viewer), the talk show host pressed them with very probing questions, and in each case their "explanations" under questioning did not match up with their carefully crafted opening statements. In other words, their public relations face and their real agenda are two separate and very different things! They are (in my judgment) lying through their (plastic-smile) teeth in an effort to con us all over again.

We must not hold still for that to happen.

Christians must rise up and speak out! Patriots who love freedom must stand against the tyranny of Islam!

Islam Incompatible With Christianity

Many in the aftermath of September 11 have tried to calm our feelings and fears by claiming that Muslims and Christians worship the same God. Their reasoning is that Allah and Jehovah are just two different names for the same Being. Neither Bible-believing Christians nor Koran-believing Muslims believe this. The contrast between God and Allah is easy to see. Allah is portrayed as a sovereign master, as is the God of the Bible. However, Allah remains aloof and unapproachable in his sovereignty. There is no parallel to a loving Father, a sacrificial Husband or a gentle Shepherd. The idea that God could be such is at least nearly blasphemous in the Islamic belief.

Another great difference is seen in the person of Jesus. For the Christian He is unquestionably divine, being the second Person in the Trinity; whereas to the Muslim the idea of a Trinity is polytheism. It is said by them that God could have no son because He has no wife. In their reasoning God is above humans in His being but is unable to have a son by non-human means. Jesus is regarded by them as somewhat special, being born of a virgin and chosen as a great prophet of Allah. The Koran says that Jesus was not crucified, so there would naturally have been no resurrection.

This would leave us with no Redeemer and no payment for our sins; but this does not really matter to them, since salvation, according to Islam, is by our own works anyway. Surah 7:8,9 and Surah 23:102,103 both present the judgment as the weighing of works in a balance with those gaining Paradise whose good works are sufficiently heavy. The Islamic definition of good works includes the repetition that there is no god but Allah and Muham-mad is his prophet, praying five times daily in the direction of Mecca, giving one-fortieth of one's possessions as alms, fasting during daylight hours during the month of Ramadan each year and attempting to make a pilgrimage to Mecca at least once during one's lifetime. There is no security for them in all this because there is no certainty of the works being sufficient. Those behind the violence would add that martyrdom in battle would guarantee a reward in Paradise, but this is not one of the five basic works of most Muslims.

While Islam labels the Bible as corrupt, it borrows freely from it. Hundreds of Koran references can be traced directly to the Bible, as, for example, the various mentions of Abraham, Moses and Jesus. Of course, the Koran offers its own twist on each such thing. In reference to creation, the Koran says, variously, that it took two days (41:9, 12), then four days (41:10), and then six days (7:54; 10:3; 11:7; 25:59). Either Allah's memory is faulty or Muhammad's hearing is impaired!

Islam, like the Koran, was the invention of a madman named Muhammad. His personal life, as well as his recorded teaching, exposes him for a very strange individual.

Muhammad had seventeen wives, including one six-year-old child-bride. In civilized society he would be considered a child molester. He took his adopted son's wife as his own, but only after getting permission in a special vision from Gabriel. Caught in immorality with a slave girl, once again Gabriel conveniently gave license. Gibbon, the historian, described him as an "illiterate barbarian." We heartily concur!

While Muslims tout the Koran and the Hadith as holy books with no human source, both are nonetheless strange documents and very inconsistent ones.

From the Koran and the Hadith a picture of Islamic beliefs emerges which includes:

(1) a very impersonal god, no saviour, no mediator, no forgiveness of sins, a code of "good works" as the avenue to Heaven; and the only absolute assurance of Heaven is contained in suicide missions to kill unbelievers.

(2) the idea that Jesus was a mere man, a teacher and a prophet, but not God! They totally reject any idea of His deity and dispute the claims of the crucifixion and resurrection.

(3) their lack of confidence in the Scriptures. Although they believe that portions of the Bible—namely, the Torah, the Psalms and the Gospels—were inspired, they insist that it has now been "corrupted," thus creating the necessity for looking elsewhere. Conveniently, they are ready with the

Koran since, they say, the Bible text is no longer reliable.

(4) their rejection of the concepts of the love of God and of the judgment of God. Everything hinges on the "good works" of a person outweighing his "bad works." Apparently, only a slight edge of good more than evil or evil more than good will determine the eternal outcome of a Muslim.

(5) their belief that

> "If God wants you, He will have you; and if He doesn't want you, He does want you to go to Hell. That is fatalism. That's what Islam teaches: that God pleases to damn people as much as He pleases to let them into Heaven by their good works. He wants them to be damned. He, in His will, causes them to be damned," [said Emir Caner who at the age of 12 became a Christian after having been a Muslim. His uncles, cousins and two sisters live as Muslims. His father died a Muslim].

> The underlying theological current of Islam is that of fatalism (*Baptist Press*).

(6) their inclination toward militancy. Muslims who take the Koran seriously are not prone toward peace but rather are inclined to take up the chant and cry of the *jihad* (holy war).

> "We must never imagine that such Muslims are being unnecessarily wicked. They are simply being faithful to their religion. The fact is never hidden as to the attitude a good Muslim should have towards Christians and Jews. In fact, much of the incitement to violence and war in the whole of the Koran is directed against the Jews and Christians who rejected what they felt to be the strange god Muhammad was trying to preach," [said] former Muslim and Islamic scholar G. J. O. Moshay (*Who Is This Allah?* Dorchester House Publications, 1994, p. 24).

> The Hadith calls *jihad* [holy war]—"the best method of earning [blessings] both spiritual and temporal. If victory is won, there is enormous booty of a country, which cannot be equaled to any other source of income. If there is defeat or death, there is everlasting paradise" (*Mishkat Masabih*, Volume II, p. 253).

One thing has become clear to us: The holy books of Islam teach violence against non-Muslims. If an individual Muslim does not take up the cause of *jihad* (holy war), it is simply because he chooses to ignore portions of the Koran.

There is no comparable passage in the [Christian] New Testament. It would be impossible to find in the life of Jesus either precedent or approval of taking political hostages or assassination or any other barbarism. No normally intelligent spokesman for the Christian Faith would try to justify such actions—certainly not with a New Testament in hand (C. Donald Cole, *Christian Perspectives on the News*, 3/17/96).

There Is a Difference Between Islam and Christianity

In Islam, the followers of Allah go on missions to kill themselves and to kill others so that they can go to Heaven. In Christianity, God sent His Son, Jesus Christ, to die on behalf of the human race so that all of us through Him could live now and forever. What a difference!

In Islam, the shedding of blood is so common as to be routine. The slaughter of innocents, millions of them, can be traced all the way to Muhammad himself. The taking of blood has been a way of life in Islam. In Christianity, God the Father sent His Son, Jesus Christ, to shed His blood for us. His sacrifice was a "once for all" (Heb. 10:10) atonement. As a result, Christians defend and protect life.

Those who dare compare Muslim terrorism with the Crusades and claim that Christians are guilty of such atrocities are ignorant of history. The Crusades took place during the Dark Ages—called such because people were illiterate and not taught the Scripture, hence the "dark" age.

The Crusades took place when a large number of non-Christian...Roman Catholics followed the orders of a few demon-possessed popes. They trudged through Europe raping and killing Jews AND Muslims in an effort to conquer the Holy Land for purely POLITICAL purposes. These were not "Christian terrorists."

They were anti-Christian, Roman Catholic terrorists. They did what they did IN SPITE OF the life and teachings of Jesus Christ. Muslim terrorists do what they do AS A RESULT OF the life and teachings of Muhammad. In Muslim nations where Sharia, or Islamic Law, has been adopted, non-Muslims are persecuted, detained and even KILLED every single day (G. A. Miller, www.outofseason.com).

There is not one Christian nation on earth where Muslims

are persecuted. Yet in 83% of nations where the majority of the population are Muslims, there is systematic government persecution of Christians (*Conservative Truth*).

In Islam, the disciples torture and kill "unbelievers," but in Christianity, the perspectives and the practices are decidedly pro-life! In Islam, repression and tyranny are germane to its very existence, while in Christianity, freedom is a principal factor.

Chapter Five

Witnessing to Muslims and Winning Them to Christ

The people from across the world who have embraced Islam are very real people. They live and they die just like everyone else. They have families, they get sick, they work to make a living, they ponder the issues of life—just like all the rest of us.

Muslims Need Our Witness

Despite the cultural, racial, ethnic, economic, political and numerous other differences, these are real people with real needs and with real life concerns. They face the struggles of life, the contemplations of death and the uncertainties of eternity wanting answers.

Inside the Muslim culture there is not a flow of information; consequently, most Muslims have not been exposed to anything except the Islamic propaganda. They have no personal, intimate knowledge of God, since Allah is portrayed as a sovereign tyrant to whom they must submit or be forever doomed. The idea of God as a loving Father who cares personally about them is totally foreign.

Furthermore, the Muslim disciple has no Saviour on whom he can totally rely. There is no assurance of sins forgiven. For them there is no guarantee of ultimate salvation. The Muslim must daily confess that "There is one god; his name is Allah; and Muhammad is his prophet."

Even then, the confession is always within a context of uncertainty. The Muslim cannot know that he is on solid ground with God. He has no promise that assures—in fact, no

assurance at all. He has only a hope that his works will sufficiently please Allah and then perhaps he will be given some
status in Paradise one day.

When you connect these eternal insecurities with the climate of fear, repression and tyranny where the average
Muslim has been born and reared, indeed, where he lives his
whole life, then add the hostility which he is incessantly fed
toward everything non-Islamic, it creates a very difficult shell
around the Muslim's heart and mind.

Reaching Muslims with the truth is at best a difficult task
and one which has seen very limited success. However, it
must be admitted that there has been very little investment
made in this effort. The Islam-dominated countries are virtu-
ally closed to Christian missionary efforts. The tyrants who
rule those countries are harshly unmerciful toward those who
bear a witness and will go so far as inflicting imprisonment
and execution. They are equally as ruthless toward their own
people who receive a witness. Even to possess a gospel tract
could result in the sternest of penalties—perhaps death.

The Muslims in America are not typically living under such
tyranny, but their ethnic and religious culture is a very isolated and closed one. Even in the Islamic mosques in America,
the indoctrination is fierce. Anything non-Muslim is treated
as an alien, an apostate and an adversary. So, by the very
structure and spirit of their socio-religio-politico-ethnic culture, they are indoctrinated against anything and everything
non-Islamic.

Recently, however, we have seen a few reports which indicate that the events of September 11 have not set well with
some within Islam. The graphic images from television of the
hate and hostility, including the arbitrary killing of thousands
of innocent people, have not gone unnoticed by all of them.
Some of them are suddenly brought face-to-face with the
harsh realities generated by the disciples of Islam. Questions
without answers are in their minds now. September 11 has left
indelible shadows of uncertainty. Doubts about Allah, the
Koran, the Hadith and the whole Islamic philosophy have sur-
faced because of these murderous and catastrophic attacks.

As the facts have become known, we have learned it was

not just Americans and not just Christians and Jews who died on September 11. Victims in the World Trade Center Towers were from eighty-six different nations, and many of them were Muslims.

If Osama bin Laden and his warriors were truly carrying out the will of Allah on September 11th, if they were simply exterminating the infidels (non-Muslims), then why did they also murder a good number of Muslims in those Towers? How does a Muslim family reconcile the death of their son or daughter who was merely going about his/her business and just happened to be in one of the Towers when the airplanes hit them? These questions may be sidestepped by the cold, calculating spinmeisters of Islam, but in the grief-filled hearts of these families there will be doubt.

So, in these times, we must not hesitate to do the job which needs to be done. We must stand up, and we must speak the truth. We must courageously and compassionately give the witness of the Gospel.

How to Witness to Muslims

Here are some pointers that we believe will help:

(1) Remember that the Word of God is not the same as the word of man. The Bible is not the Koran. Amen!

"For the word of God is quick, and powerful, and sharper than any twoedged sword, piercing even to the dividing asunder of soul and spirit, and of the joints and marrow, and is a discerner of the thoughts and intents of the heart."—Heb. 4:12.

"And that from a child thou hast known the holy scriptures, which are able to make thee wise unto salvation through faith which is in Christ Jesus.

"All scripture is given by inspiration of God, and is profitable for doctrine, for reproof, for correction, for instruction in righteousness."—II Tim. 3:15,16.

Whether a Muslim believes the Bible or not, we must unashamedly and without flinching present it to him. The Word of God is powerful, but we must get it presented so that its power can work.

"So shall my word be that goeth forth out of my mouth: it shall

not return unto me void, but it shall accomplish that which I please, and it shall prosper in the thing whereto I sent it."—Isa. 55:11.

"So then faith cometh by hearing, and hearing by the word of God."—Rom. 10:17.

Christians must not forget that the Word of God is unlike anything else. When we fail to proclaim it, there is no possibility for success. Some of the seed sown may not fall on good ground (Matt. 13), but we must keep on sowing it.

In witnessing to Muslims, don't surrender your weapon! The Bible is the Word of God, and the Word of God is provocative, penetrating and powerful!

"For I am not ashamed of the gospel of Christ: for it is the power of God unto salvation to every one that believeth; to the Jew first, and also to the Greek."—Rom. 1:16.

(2) Prepare yourself in prayer. As in every other situation where we encounter an unsaved person, we are best prepared if we ready ourselves in prayer before the Lord, claiming His power for the success of our witness. Ask the Lord for His protection and for His peace within yourself, as well as for His power upon the Word and upon you.

Remember, this is a spiritual battle! The enemy is very real! We must approach our witness with full awareness that we are entering into hostile territory where conflict is raging!

"For we wrestle not against flesh and blood, but against principalities, against powers, against the rulers of the darkness of this world, against spiritual wickedness in high places."—Eph. 6:12.

"For though we walk in the flesh, we do not war after the flesh:

"(For the weapons of our warfare are not carnal, but mighty through God to the pulling down of strong holds;)

"Casting down imaginations, and every high thing that exalteth itself against the knowledge of God, and bringing into captivity every thought to the obedience of Christ."—II Cor. 10:3–5.

(3) See each Muslim as an individual! Each one is a very real person. Each one is a precious soul. Each one is one for whom Christ died on the cross. Each one is the victim of a false system that has duped him or her into a deception that is very deep.

"All we like sheep have gone astray; we have turned every one to his own way; and the LORD hath laid on him the iniquity of us all."—Isa. 53:6.

"And the Word was made flesh, and dwelt among us, (and we beheld his glory, the glory as of the only begotten of the Father,) full of grace and truth."—John 1:14.

Establishing the fact of their true need and the real truth about each one of them should be done with Scripture. Show it to them and then read it aloud. Read it slowly and deliberately.

They need to be told that they are known to God and that He cares personally for them.

"For God so loved the world, that he gave his only begotten Son, that whosoever believeth in him should not perish, but have everlasting life.

"For God sent not his Son into the world to condemn the world; but that the world through him might be saved.

"He that believeth on him is not condemned: but he that believeth not is condemned already, because he hath not believed in the name of the only begotten Son of God."—John 3:16–18.

(4) Approach your witness confidently, aggressively and, yes, boldly.

A weak, hesitating, apologetic approach will not get far with Muslims. A firm but friendly presentation is required when working with them. You must be confident of your message and present it aggressively (not forcefully) and boldly (not brashly).

Be prepared to show them that the Koran is fallible and historically deficient.

(5) Familiarize yourself sufficiently with Islam so that you are not intimidated by the facade with which they face you.

(6) Ask for a hearing, an opportunity to present your case! "Has anyone ever sat down with you to show you the claims of Christ and the full story of the Gospel of Christ?" Whatever their answer, ask them if you can do it!

Try to arrange your setting so as not to be where the Muslim is under the gazing eyes of one or more of his Muslim family or friends. Otherwise, the "peer" pressure may doom your efforts from the start.

(7) Stay at it over a period of time! "Can we talk again?" "Could we visit together again next week?" Keep the door open and keep talking!

It's not likely that you will win very many Muslims with one presentation each. There's a lot to overcome, and you have to be committed to a patient and persistent witness.

Concluding Appeal

Folks, nap time is over! Our sleeping churches must awaken and recommit themselves to the Great Commission of Christ (Matt. 28:19,20).

The threat of Islam is very real! It is a threat to our faith, to our country and to our personal safety.

Freedom and free enterprise are at stake. Our way of life provokes the antagonism and hostility of Islam. We must not dialogue with Islam as though it were some ideology with which we can fraternize. It is not!

We must preach Christ! We must herald the truths of the Bible.

We must evangelize aggressively inside the Islamic culture. The eternal destiny of the millions within Islam hinges upon our efforts.

Now is the time; we must not linger! To delay simply allows the already "raging storm" to intensify, to gather more strength.

Revised Edition
Chapters 6–9

Since the Islamic terrorists attacked America on September 11, 2001, we have had dozens of Islam-related news items in the SWORD OF THE LORD newspaper.

We have included many of them in the next four chapters, because in a very real way the events continued to expose the true nature of Islam as well as the radical agenda of its most devoted followers.

Chapter Six
Persecution of Christians in Islamic Countries

I. Middle Eastern Countries:

A. Saudi Arabia

Christians Remain in Saudi Jail (3/29/02)

ABU DHABI—Saudi Arabia has refused a U.S. appeal to release more than a dozen Christians accused of practicing their faith. The Christians were arrested in a series of raids that began in July in the Saudi city of Jedda. U.S. diplomats raised the issue...and were told that the Christians would be released....

The practice of any other religion but Islam is banned by Saudi law. Over the last decade, Saudi authorities had allowed private prayer but...cracked down on non-Islamic practice during the [recent] Muslim fast month of Ramadan.

—Middle East Newsline

Two Christians Deported From Saudi Arabia (8/16/02)

Two Filipino men who were caught in possession of a Bible and some Christian CDs when police raided their room in March 2001 in Saudi Arabia have been deported to the Philippines. A local court had sentenced [them] to a month's imprisonment in April 2001, and a higher court increased their sentence to include 150 lashes in January 2002....The men were spared the lashes but were deported...instead.

—*RELIGION TODAY*

EDITOR'S COMMENTS: This is in the Islamically ruled Saudi Arabia. The

Saudis are one of the moderate Muslim regimes who profess to be friends to the U.S. But as in all the Islam-dominated countries, freedom is limited, and religious freedom is not at all!

Saudi Arabia Islamic Government Totally Intolerant of Christians (6/20/03)

Two Africans jailed in the port city of Jeddah for "Christian activities" are due to be deported. After first revoking residence permits for Girmaye Ambaye, 44, of Eritrea, and Endeshawe Adana Yizengaw, 32, of Ethiopia, police arrested and jailed them recently, Compass Direct reported....

"The reason they are sending us back is that we are Christians," Yizengaw said....Yizengaw has been called in for questioning by the police several times over the last two years and accused of selling alcohol and being involved in prostitution, helping the U.S. government spread Christianity and trying to convert Muslims.

The U.S. Commission on Religious Freedom's annual report on the status of religious liberties worldwide, released [May 13], cited Saudi Arabia as the top violator, the Washington Times reported.

—CNS

Saudi Arabia Deports Eritrean Christian (9/26/03)

After 20 weeks in a Saudi jail for participating in prohibited Christian activities, Eritrean Christian Girmaye Ambaye was deported from Jeddah by plane back to his home country on Saturday, August 9....Ambaye had been jailed at the Bremen deportation center in the Saudi port city of Jeddah since March 25, when local police put him under arrest for talking to Muslim Arabs about his Christian faith....Ambaye is one of a dozen members of an Ethiopian-Eritrean Christian congregation in Jeddah who have been jailed and deported. Jeddah police keep church leaders under frequent surveillance.

—RELIGION TODAY

Saudi Arabia Added to Religious Freedom Watch List (12/3/04)

The U.S. State Department on September 15 for the first time included Saudi Arabia on a list of eight "countries of particular concern" for not allowing religious freedom, a potential stumbling block for relations between the United States and its Persian Gulf ally.

The department's sixth annual report on international religious freedom also added Eritrea and Vietnam to the roster of those countries guilty or tolerant of "systematic, ongoing, egregious violations of religious freedom."

Countries that remained on the list were Burma, China, Iran, North Korea and Sudan. Iraq, which had been on the list under Saddam Hussein's regime, was removed.

—BAPTISTS TODAY

Religious Freedom Watchdog Wants U.S. to Act Against Saudi Arabia (4/8/05)

A religious freedom organization is urging Secretary of State Condoleezza Rice to impose travel and other restrictions on Saudi Arabia within the next month because of severe freedom of religion violations in the kingdom.

Having last year designated Saudi Arabia a "country of particular concern" because of its abuses, the State Department is required by March 15 to take specific steps, the U.S. Commission on International Religious Freedom (USCIRF) told Rice in a letter this week.

The commission, a body set up under the International Religious Freedom Act, says Saudi Arabia strictly prohibits all public religious expression other than those that follow the government's interpretation of Islam.

Violations include torture, cruel and degrading treatment, detention without charge, coercive measures aimed at women, and the wide jurisdiction of the religious police.

The kingdom also is accused of funding or otherwise supporting the spreading abroad of an ideology of hatred, intolerance and violence.

—RELIGION TODAY

Saudis Shred Bibles, Rights Campaigners Claim (7/15/05)

Bibles found in the possession of visitors to Saudi Arabia are routinely confiscated by customs officials, and in some cases copies allegedly have been put through a paper shredder, according to religious rights campaigners.

Reports from the Islamic world of the abuse of Bibles and other items important to Christians emerge from time to time but generally have little impact—in contrast to the wave of Muslim anger sparked by a Newsweek report, since retracted, of Koran desecration by the U.S. military.

Danny Nalliah, a Sri Lankan-born evangelical pastor, [said], "It's a very well-known fact that if you have a Bible at customs when you enter the airport, and if they find the Bible, the Bible is taken and put in the shredder."

"If you have more than one Bible, you will be taken into custody; and if you have a quantity of Bibles, you will be given 70 lashes for sure—you could even be executed."

—RELIGION TODAY

Saudi Police Arrest Forty Foreigners Proselytizing (7/15/05)

Forty foreigners, including children, were arrested for proselytizing when police raided a clandestine church in suburban Riyadh. Lt. Col. Saad al-Rashud said the forty were arrested [April 22] in Badeea neighborhood.

It is illegal to promote religions other than Islam in Saudi Arabia, the birthplace of Islam. There are no legal churches in the conservative kingdom, where members of other religions generally can practice their faith in their own homes but not try to convert people or hold religious gatherings.

A conviction on proselytizing can result in a harsh prison sentence followed by deportation.

—JERUSALEM POST

Saudi Arabia Conducts Worst Crackdown on Christians in Decade (8/12/05)

Saudi Arabian police have made a wave of arrests of Christians since May 27, constituting the largest crackdown on followers of Christ in the Muslim-dominated country in the last decade, according to a Washington-based human rights organization. International Christian Concern reported it had learned of 46 confirmed arrests...through June 1....It...has confirmed reports of police ransacking the houses of Christians and destroying Bibles, ICC reported.

Regular Saudi police and Muttawa religious police have carried out these actions....Saudi Arabia is listed by the U.S. State

Department as one of the world's most severe violators of religious freedom. Last year, the State Department placed Saudi Arabia on its list of "countries of particular concern" for the first time. The CPC designation is reserved for governments that have "engaged in or tolerated systemic and egregious violations of religious freedom."

—RELIGION TODAY

Saudis Release Christian Detainees (8/12/05)

Saudi officials...announced the release of seven Christians who had been arrested for practicing Christianity in the Kingdom. Of the released, six were arrested on May 28 in an extensive raid carried out by the Muttawa in Riyadh....

In Saudi Arabia, public expression of any faith other than Wahabbist Islam is illegal. All seven had been caught with Christian items—including Bibles, crosses and teaching materials. Their release was contingent upon each Christian signing a renunciation to non-Muslim religious practice, which they had been carrying out privately in their homes....

A Saudi official speaking in Cairo denied allegations that the Kingdom arrests and tortures Christians....

After their release, local press sources—referring to telephone calls from the prison—reported that the Christian prisoners were subjected to abuse....

...Saudi Arabia has its own religious police, the Muttawa, who have a reputation for violations of religious freedom for non-Muslims.

—Institute on Religion and Public Policy

EDITOR'S COMMENTS: Of course, the official rhetoric is denial, but the facts are undeniable. Simply put—where Islam is in control, abusive religious intolerance is widely practiced!

B. Egypt

Christian Converts From Islam Imprisoned in Egypt (8/29/03)

A Christian couple has spent months in prison because of the wife's conversion. Naglaa, a Christian convert from Islam, and her husband, Malak Gawargios Fahmy, were imprisoned in mid-February in an effort to force Naglaa to give up her Christian faith. The pair was arrested at the airport as they tried to leave Egypt for Cyprus....

"Becoming Christian shouldn't be a crime punishable by a prison sentence," Egyptian church leaders said. "It is strictly forbidden to convert from Islam to Christianity....Freedom of religion should be a human right to all, and conversions should take place with each person's own accord."

—RELIGION TODAY

Egypt Cracks Down Against Converts to Christianity (12/19/03)

In a harsh crackdown [October 10–20], Egypt's state security police...arrested and tortured a Christian couple from Muslim background, along with eleven other Egyptian citizens accused of forging Christian identity papers for former Muslims. At least ten more Christians have since been detained and subjected to torture in the sweep, said to be headed by two security police officers known for illegal and cruel tactics against Christian converts. The convert couple—Mohammed Ahmed Imam Kordy and his wife, Sahar El-Sayed Abdel Ghany—were arrested in Alexandria on October 18. The police action apparently came after the wife was implicated in a complaint extorted under police torture that she had helped another Egyptian woman secure false identity papers.

—RELIGION TODAY

EDITOR'S COMMENTS: Once again Islam shows itself ugly and tyrannical where it has a dominance in the government. Egypt officially has been quite friendly to the United States, but with Islam so strong, one must always be leery.

Couple Escapes Muslim Persecution in Egypt (6/18/04)

Thirteen months after Egypt jailed and tortured a Coptic Christian pharmacist for marrying a former Muslim woman, Boulos Farid Rezek-Allah Awad was finally allowed to emigrate from Egypt to Canada in March. A few weeks earlier, his wife, Enas Yehya Abdel Aziz, had escaped the country to claim refugee status abroad. Egyptian security police officials told Rezek-Allah last November that he was permanently blacklisted from leaving Egypt; they vowed to track down and punish his wife for her "illegal" marriage to a Christian.

—RELIGION TODAY

C. Yemen

Three Southern Baptist Missionaries Martyred, Probably by Muslim (1/17/03)

Dr. Martha Myers,...57, was one of three Southern Baptist missionaries killed by a gunman [December 30] in the Yemeni town of Jibla. The gunman walked into the hospital where the three were in a meeting and shot them in the head.

Also killed were the hospital's director, William Koehn, 60, of Arlington, Texas, and its business manager, Kathleen Gariety, 53, of Wauwatosa, Wisconsin.

—USA TODAY

Yemeni Man Testifies That He Killed American Missionaries (5/23/03)

(RNS)—A Yemeni man suspected of having ties to al-Qaida has testified that he killed three American missionaries at a Southern Baptist hospital because he believed they were trying to convert Muslims. Abed Abdul Razak Kamel told a court in Jibla, Yemen, on Sunday (April 20) that he planned the December 30 attack for a year and a half, the Associated Press reported. "I acted out of a religious duty...and in revenge for those who converted Muslims from their religion and made them unbelievers," said Kamel at the opening of his trial in southern Yemen....Kamel...testified he traveled to Jibla in July 2001 and began to scout his target by frequently visiting the hospital and asking about its activities. "I found out that they were truly converting Muslims into Christians," he said. Residents of Jibla have said the Americans working at the hospital never discussed religion. Yemeni law bars non-Muslims from proselytizing in the country, which is overwhelmingly Muslim.

D. Sudan

Sudanese Islamic Government Ongoing Assault on Christians (3/29/02)

"To be a Christian in Sudan is a matter of survival and not living," says Hamilton Lugar with Voice of the Martyrs. "Christian families in the Sudan often can't tell who will be next in the line of fire....

"There is no freedom of worship, no equality, as our young boys are denied education," Lugar told Religion Today. "And those who are lucky enough to reach colleges are forced into the military before they get their certificates. Most are sent to southern Sudan where the war is dragging on, to fight against their fellow Southerners. Few return. Young girls are raped by Sudanese soldiers, and children are enslaved. Churches, schools and hospitals are burnt."

This is life...for Sudan's two million Christians....

Sudanese Christians have been persecuted since the mid-1950s, but a cease-fire held through the '70s. In 1983, the Islamic government came to power and replaced the Sudanese constitution with one based on Islamic law and an emphasis on the military. "Jihad" (holy war) was officially declared against the Southern "infidels."...

According to Steve Snyder with International Christian Concern, "The tensions in Sudan are due to the radical, militant Islamic regime that has pledged to Islamize all Africa. The regime has been responsible for nearly two million deaths over the past eighteen years and the massacre of the mostly Christian population in the South. Therefore, it is no surprise that the regime will not tolerate Christians' becoming too vocal about their faith in public, probably because some Muslims have become Christians."

—RELIGION TODAY

Muslim Regimes Intolerant of Anything Christian (6/18/04)

The Islamic regime in Khartoum recently lashed and fined a Christian woman for not wearing a head scarf in public in the capital city. On April 14, Cecilia John Holland, 27, was traveling by minibus to her home in the Khartoum suburb of Haj Yousif when she was arrested by a group of 10 policemen, Compass Direct reported.

She was given 40 lashes on her back and fined the equivalent of $40 by an Islamic court. The police told Holland that no one in Khartoum, "even a non-Muslim," was exempt from Islamic bans against wearing improper dress.

Last month, the Khartoum government refused to compromise on its insistence that Islamic law govern all Sudanese citizens residing in the city, Compass reported. More than 2 million non-Muslim southerners live in and around the capital, displaced by the last 20 years of civil war between the African Christian-animist south and the Arab Muslim north.

—charismanow.com

E. United Arab Emirates

United Arab Emirates Charges Baptist Pastor With a "Felony" (6/6/03)

A criminal court has found a Filipino pastor guilty of "abusing Islam" and conducting missionary activity, but a judge dismissed his yearlong jail sentence. Arrested five months ago for giving a Bible and Christian literature to an Arab Muslim at a Dubai shopping center, Fernando Alconga was held in jail for five weeks and charged with a felony for "preaching other than the Islamic religion," as forbidden in the Federal Criminal Code, Compass Direct reported.

Eight court hearings were conducted in his trial, which opened in January. In a verdict reached earlier..., Chief Judge Mahmood Fahmi Sultan suspended Alconga's punishment because the court believed that the 54-year-old pastor would not repeat his crime....Alconga [is]...an ordained Conservative Baptist minister who has pastored congregations in the United Arab Emirates for the last nine years.

—CNS

EDITOR'S COMMENTS: How nice of the Muslim judge to let the pastor go free, since he doesn't think he will do it again! Actually, the pastor is moving to the Philippines to pastor a church there! Here is another case of how Islam and its adherents behave when they have dominance in the government!

F. Turkmenistan

Religious Persecution in Turkmenistan (11/21/03)

Police recently banned members of a Baptist congregation from meeting for services, threatening them with fines if they continued to meet. The raid occurred late [in August] during a Sunday service in the town of Balkanabad....

The church has been targeted for several raids this year. Church leaders have complained that all its members were fined the equivalent of $48 each for gathering for...services in July and August....

Turkmenistan has the harshest religious policy of all the former Soviet republics....Authorities recognize no faiths except for the officially sanctioned Muslim religion and the Russian Orthodox Church.

—CNS

G. Turkey

Turkish Churches Ordered to Close (4/26/02)

Compass Direct reports that the Turkish Interior Ministry ordered local authorities in nine provinces to investigate the "legality" of some 40 small Protestant churches. According to Compass, provincial police authorities began in late November to deliver formal notifications..., declaring that their rented or purchased places of worship are in violation of municipal building laws....

Turkey's population of 66 million is mostly Muslim.

—RELIGION TODAY

H. Tajikistan

Baptist Leader Shot Dead While Praying (3/12/04)

A Baptist leader was shot dead while praying in a chapel in the Central Asian Muslim nation of Tajikistan.

Sergei Bessarab, a missionary in the town of Isfar, was shot with an automatic weapon by an unidentified assailant....

He was shot 13 times with a Kalashnikov assault rifle, an official from the United Nations office in Dushanbe said....

A Norway-based persecution watchdog group, Forum 18, said the pastor's active missionary work—which included distributing Tajik-language evangelistic booklets—had aroused the anger of some local people.

One week before his death, the local paper Nasimi Isfara published an article sharply criticizing Bessarab's missionary work, Forum 18 said....

Christians comprise an estimated one percent of Tajikistan's seven million people. About 90 percent are Muslims.

—WorldNetDaily

I. Lebanon

Jordanian Christian Killed in Lebanon Attack (6/20/03)

ISTANBUL (Compass, May 7)—An Arab convert to Christianity was killed in a bomb blast last night outside his Tripoli apartment, adjacent to the home of a European missionary family thought to have been targeted in the attack.

Jamil Ahmed al-Rifai, 28, died instantly when a bomb exploded just before midnight in the Qubba suburb of Tripoli, Lebanon's northern port city.

Despite reports on the Qatar-based Al-Jazeera television network that al-Rifai had himself planted the bomb, eyewitnesses confirmed that the Jordanian Christian was an innocent victim of the attack.

...Al-Rifai left Jordan in 1997 "because of pressure from the authorities over his conversion to Christianity."...

The deadly Tripoli bombing was the second attack against Christian missionaries in Lebanon in the past six months.

—RELIGION TODAY

J. Iraq

Outspoken Christian Convert Murdered in Iraq (4/11/03)

CNS—A Christian convert threatened repeatedly for turning his back on Islam has been murdered. Ismaeel Mohamad Ismaeel died [February 24] in Zakho, in the northern Kurdistan region, when he was killed by a man wielding a machine gun, Open Doors-Australia said....Friends say that Ismaeel's increasing openness about his faith had caused growing tension with local Muslims. A taxi driver, Ismaeel,...after his second arrest,...was told by police "some people did not like that he was witnessing about Christ," Open Doors said. After his conversion, Ismaeel was declared an apostate by a local mullah and abducted by relatives who threatened to kill him if he did not renounce Christianity. He was rescued and taken into hiding by Christian friends, but returned to open life...."I have to go back to my family to tell them that even when they kill me, I will never deny Christ." Ismaeel leaves a wife and five children.

—RELIGION TODAY

K. Iran

Iranian Pastor Faces Execution (7/1/05)

[A]...lay pastor, who became a Christian 25 years ago, faces execution by hanging under Islamic law for leaving the Muslim faith. Hamid Pourmand, 47, has been on trial for his life for several days before a shari'a court in Tehran for deserting Islam and proselytizing Muslims, Compass Direct reported.

However, authorities abandoned the hearings against Pourmand..., apparently after news of his trial leaked out to the international press.

—charismanow.com

II. Other Asian Countries:

A. Pakistan

Pakistan Islamic Laws Persecute Christians (4/26/02)

A high court in the nation's eastern region has upheld a decision sentencing two Christian men to life in prison for allegedly burning the Quran....

The defendants, convicted of blasphemy in the city of Lahore, have argued that police set them up after they refused to pay a bribe, said Bhatti [president of the All-Pakistan Minorities Alliance]....

Under Pakistan's blasphemy laws, those who desecrate the Quran, offend Islam or insult its prophet can be punished with death. Hundreds of people have been jailed on blasphemy convictions.

—CNS

Pakistan Acquits Illiterate Christian of Blasphemy (9/27/02)

After four and one-half years in prison for alleged blasphemy against Islam, Pakistani Christian Aslam Masih was acquitted [June 4] in a...hearing before the Lahore High Court. In his mid 50s and illiterate, Masih was arrested in November 1998 on charges that he had desecrated the Quran by hanging verses from the Muslim holy book in a charm around a dog's neck. Although the prosecution only produced hearsay evidence against Masih, he was found guilty in May 2002 and sentenced to double life sentences. In overturning Masih's lower-court conviction, Justice Najam ur-Zaman reportedly took what one observer called "a very aggressive attitude against the prosecution," noting that the prosecution's chief witness had retracted the statement attributed to him by the police. "There are a lot of threats when such a person gets acquitted and then released," one of the lawyers pointed out. Most go into strict hiding until they can be safely sent out of the country for asylum, out of the reach of extremist Muslims vowing to kill them despite their judicial acquittal. Seven other Christians remain jailed in Pakistan on drawn-out charges of blasphemy.

—RELIGION TODAY

EDITOR'S COMMENTS: The evidence continues to mount against Islam. It is NOT "a religion of peace."

Another Christian's Blasphemy Trial
Starts in Pakistan (11/22/02)

Trial proceedings against Christian schoolteacher Pervaiz Masih began on July 17 in northeast Pakistan, two years and three months after the high-school principal was jailed for alleged blasphemy. Now 35, Masih has been refused bail since his arrest in April 2001, when teenage boys reportedly claimed he had made slanderous remarks against the Muslim prophet Mohammed while tutoring them two months earlier.

—RELIGION TODAY

Islamic Militants Suspected in Church Bombing (7/4/03)

ISLAMABAD, Pakistan (AP)—A grenade attack on a Protestant church packed with Sunday worshipers killed five people—including an American woman and her daughter—in an assault clearly aimed at Pakistan's foreign community.

No group claimed responsibility for the attack, in which at least one young man...ran through the center of the church hurling grenades. But suspicion fell on Islamic extremists....

Eight other Americans were among the 45 people injured, most of whom were foreigners....

President Bush condemned the attack...and called it an act of terrorism.

—ROCKY MOUNTAIN NEWS

Pakistan Christian School Target
of Anti-West Attack (9/12/03)

MURREE, Pakistan (AP)—Gunmen firing...rifles burst through the front gates of a Christian school [August 5], killing six people and wounding three in the latest attack against Western interests since Pakistan joined the war against terrorism....

It was the sixth attack against Westerners or Western interests in Pakistan this year, most of which have been blamed on Islamic militant groups angered by President Pervez Musharraf's backing of the U.S. war on terrorism. Since October, two churches have been attacked, leaving 20 dead, including two Americans....

Police found a note at the scene expressing "resentment against world powers."

—NASHVILLE TENNESSEAN

Gunmen "Execute" Pakistani Christians (10/24/03)

Unidentified gunmen have shot dead seven people at a Christian charity in Karachi's central business district, Pakistani police say....

All those killed were Pakistani Christians.

—BBC News

Pastor and Driver Murdered in Pakistan (7/1/05)

Unknown killers kidnapped and brutally killed Protestant pastor Babar Samsoun and his driver and fellow evangelist, Daniel Emmanuel, on April 7. One of Samsoun's colleagues reported that the slain pastor as "accused of trying to convert Muslims to Christianity." the two men had been receiving telephoned threats demanding that they stop their Christian activities. Police authorities blamed the killings on an alleged family dispute.

—RELIGION TODAY

B. Philippines

U.S. Missionary Killed, Wife Wounded
During Rescue Bid (8/30/02)

An American missionary couple's year-long kidnap ordeal ended in tragedy [June 7] with one of them killed and the other wounded in a failed rescue attempt.

Martin Burnham, 42, was murdered by his abductors when Filipino troops moved in to try to free him and his wife, Gracia, from a Muslim extremist group. She was shot in the leg, while a third hostage also died in the clash near Siraway in the Philippines' southern Zamboango province.

The Burnhams and Ediborah Yapp, a Filipino nurse, were the last of a string of hostages taken by the Abu Sayyaf, an Islamic group with links to Osama bin Laden, in raids that began on May 27 last year.

New Tribes Mission, with whom the Burnhams had served in the Philippines for 16 years, said their "hearts are heavy."

—CNS

Muslims Beheaded Two Filipino Preachers (10/11/02)

Muslim guerrillas have beheaded two preachers in a grisly response to government claims that they are on the run and close to defeat. Officials said the heads were found...in the town of Patikul on southern Jolo island, two days after the Abu Sayyaf seized the two...preachers and six other hostages, Reuters reported.

"This is what will happen to those who do not believe in Allah....This is part of our jihad," said a note found near one of the [victims].

—CNS

Another American Missionary Terrorist Victim (4/25/03)

A Southern Baptist missionary was killed and another missionary and her two children were injured when a bomb exploded March 4 at the airport in Davao City, Philippines.

William P. "Bill" Hyde, 59, died in surgery from severe head and leg injuries. Barbara Wallis Stevens, 33, was slightly injured; daughter, Sarah, 4, was treated and released with minor injuries; and 10-month-old son, Nathan, also was wounded....

At least 21 people were killed and 144 injured in the attack, which occurred outside the arrival terminal of the Davao airport in the Philippines' second-largest city.

—*BAPTIST PRESS*

EDITOR'S COMMENTS: Reports have also come to us (Crosswalk) that 50 Islamic rebels stormed "a Christian village" in February on the southern Filipino island of Mindanao, killing 14 Christians, including 3 children.

Muslim Violence Targets Christian Convert (2/25/05)

A Christian who converted from Islam is recovering from serious injuries after being shot recently by Muslim activists. The twenty-four-year-old man, a fruit vendor, was shot November 17 in Zamboanga City [in the Philippines] as he took his usual route home from the market, Compass Direct reported....

The shooting victim is a member of the Tausug tribe, the first tribe in the Philippines to accept Islam and one of at least thirteen mostly Muslim tribes in the nation's southern region. Originally a Muslim, the man saw several members of his family converted after he became a Christian.

He started reaching out to others through public evangelism. This led to several death threats from Muslims in Zamboanga, who objected to his profession of faith.

...Several Muslim terrorist organizations exist in the Philippines, including the Abu Sayyaf and the Moro Islamic Liberation Front, which have been linked to Al-Qaeda.

Police sources said the groups are attracting new converts to Islam in greater numbers than Muslims born into the faith. "Converts are ideal terrorists because they are eager to prove themselves worthy of their new faith," Chief Superintendent of Police Rodolfo Mendoza said.

—charismanow.com

C. Indonesia

World's Largest Muslim Nation Has Increasing Anti-Christian Violence (3/15/02)

JAKARTA, Indonesia (PRNewswire)—The Bali bombings and the August 5 bombing of the Marriott Hotel in Jakarta highlight radical Islam's tightening grip on Indonesia. Less visible, however, is the daily terror directed at the Christian minority in the world's largest Muslim nation....

This country of 234 million people, having an 88 percent Muslim population, is a tough place for the 7 percent who are Christian or for the smaller numbers of Hindus, Buddhists and others.

An archipelago comprising some 17,000 islands, Indonesia provides not only a natural haven for terrorist groups such as Laskar Jihad and Jemaah Islamiyah, but also a backdrop for score-settling and anti-Christian violence.

A source, his name withheld for security reasons, told Christian Freedom International (CFI) what he needed to do to get a promotion: convert. "My boss told me, 'You must become a Muslim' if I want to be promoted." His employer is the government of Indonesia.

Currently, even Christians with professional credentials and advanced degrees are being denied employment and advancement in the job market.

Muslim Violence Against Churches Continues in Several Countries (3/29/02)

Muslim protestors recently attacked at least five churches. A crowd of approximately 100 people attacked the Gereja Protestan Indonesia, a Dutch Reform church, in East Bekasi [in January], Compass Direct reported.

Government officials had given permission to Christians to renovate an old house, which they had used as a church since 1975. However, leaders of the local mosque encouraged Muslims to protest against the renovations. On January 12, church members met with local government and mosque officials, agreeing to suspend renovations temporarily.

Meanwhile, three other churches were attacked on Surabaya, East Java, in December and January. Muslim protestors forced the three churches in Surabaya to close their doors. The pastor of one of the churches received death threats from the attackers. Additionally, a bomb was placed in a church in Medan, North Sumatra, Compass reported.

—CNS

Muslims Continue Killing Christians in Indonesia (7/19/02)

JAKARTA, Indonesia—A Christian leader [April 29] called for a crackdown on a paramilitary Muslim group suspected of involvement in the brutal killings of 12 Christians in Indonesia's Maluku province.

Several religious leaders said the Laskar Jihad, or Holy War Troop, was behind the attack in Soya, a Christian village on the outskirts of Maluku's provincial capital, Ambon.

The violence came two days after Laskar Jihad rejected a February peace deal meant to end the sectarian fighting in Maluku.

—*WASHINGTON TIMES*

Indonesia Muslims Commit Violence
Against Christians (10/25/02)

Muslim gunmen...shot to death five Christian men in Sulawesi....The Laskar jihad attacked the villages of Silanca and Sepe..., setting on fire several houses, the Associated Press (AP) reported.

According to witnesses, the gunmen, who wore black ninja out-fits, told Christian villagers that they would be killed if they did not leave....

"The situation in Poso has been growing more tense each day," a Sulawesi missionary [said]...."There have been bombings and shoot-ings going on regularly [against Christians]."

[Recently], 80 to 100 well-armed militants attacked the coastal Christian village of Matako, wounding seven.

—CNS

Muslim Militia Killing Christians, Burning Homes
and Churches in Indonesia (11/21/03)

JAKARTA, Indonesia (BP)—Thousands of extremist Muslim fight-ers armed with automatic weapons are attacking Christian villages in Indonesia's Central Sulawesi province, burning churches and thou-sands of homes and sending residents fleeing.

Perhaps as many as 63,000 Christians are trapped in the predom-inantly Christian city of Tentena. One missionary in Indonesia fears the "jihad warriors" will break through to Tentena and massacre the Christians who have taken refuge there.

Afghans and other foreigners are fighting alongside the Muslim militias in Sulawesi, according to news services. A policeman said he saw Muslim fighters stopping civilians at roadblocks and executing those found to be Christians....

The attacks are part of a campaign by Muslim extremists to drive out Christians from the parts of Indonesia where they are a majority and to turn Indonesia into a strict Islamic state. The country's con-stitution guarantees freedom of religion. While 88 percent of the pop-ulation is Muslim, Christians constitute an 8 percent minority and in some places are the majority.

EDITOR'S COMMENTS: If Islam is a "religion of peace," they have a

strange way of expressing it! It is not, of course! The track record of their history has been one of tyranny, coercion, violence and murder! September 11 was no isolated incident. It got our attention because it was on our doorstep! Hopefully, the civilized world is gradually coming awake to the realization that Islam is barbaric and demonic!

UN Urged to Protect Christians, Other Minorities Against Violence (3/26/04)

Christians from troubled parts of Indonesia were among a group of some 100 persecuted people from around the world who participated in a rally outside United Nations headquarters....They urged the world body to act against what they called "jihad violence" against non-Muslim minorities and Muslim moderates.

—RELIGION TODAY

Christian Leader Beheaded in Sulawesi (2/25/05)

The head of a Christian chief of the Pinedapa village [Indonesia] was found November 5 near a gas station in Poso City, Jubilee Campaign reported. Bystanders saw someone throw the head of Sarminalis Ndele, 48, from a dark vehicle. His body was found later that day. The United Kingdom-based human-rights group said the murder is the latest violence against Christians in central Sulawesi. Two pastors were shot dead in their churches, and a Christian woman was stabbed to death in front of her home. "Islamic extremists in central Sulawesi have long been trying to provoke a renewed round of Muslim-Christian conflict by repeatedly attacking Christians," said Wilfred Wong, Jubilee Campaign's researcher and parliamentary officer. He said Ndele's beheading may have been inspired by the killings in Iraq.

—CHARISMA

D. Malaysia

Bible Ban in Southeast Asian Democracy (5/23/03)

As Christians around the world prepare to mark their most important holiday, hundreds of thousands of believers in southeast Asia face the prospect of celebrating Easter without free access to the Bible.

...[The] government in Kuala Lumpur—which considers itself one of Asia's more successful democracies—has banned the Bible in their native tongue.

The Iban, the largest of 27 indigenous ethnic groups in Sarawak province on Borneo island, have since 1988 had access to the entire Bible in their own language, published by the Bible Society of Malaysia.

But now the mainly Muslim government's Home Ministry has named the Iban-language Bible as one of 35 publications it is banning because they are considered "detrimental to public peace."...

Anyone found guilty of breaching the ban faces up to three years in jail, fines of up to $5,200 or both....

Islam is Malaysia's official religion, although the federal constitution guarantees the right of all citizens to profess, practice and propagate their religion.

That freedom is subject to another clause saying that laws "may control or restrict the propagation of any religious doctrine or belief among persons professing the religion of Islam."

Critics say this provision provides the authorities with a loophole, for example, by identifying publications they can claim cause confusion among Muslims.

—RELIGION TODAY

EDITOR'S COMMENTS: Here is another example of Islam's intolerance of others. In this case, it shows clearly that even in a democracy where Islam is in the majority, they find ways to oppress.

Americans Accused of Giving Christian Pamphlets to Muslims (5/20/05)

Two Americans have been arrested in Malaysia, accused of handing out Christian pamphlets to Muslims in a country where constitutionally protected religious freedom periodically collides with Islam's stance on apostasy.

A Royal Malaysian Police spokesman said...the two men had been apprehended while handing out pamphlets outside the mosque in Putrajaya, Malaysia's new administrative capital south of Duala Lumpur....

At a brief court appearance the pair were remanded in custody for 14 days, giving authorities time "to facilitate the investigations."...

Some 60 percent of Malaysia's population are Malay Muslims, while large ethnic Chinese and Indian minorities practice Christianity and other religions.

Despite being multicultural, Sunni Islam is the official religion. Muslims are not permitted to convert to another religion.

"The constitution provides for freedom of religion; however, it recognizes Islam as the country's official religion, and the practice of Islamic beliefs other than Sunni Islam is significantly restricted," the State Department says in its most recent report on global religious freedom.

—RELIGION TODAY

E. Uzbekistan

Uzbekistan Cracks Down on Baptists (8/27/04)

Uzbekistan's secret service is interrogating and "beating up" Baptists as authorities of this mainly Islamic oriented ex-Soviet Republic are trying to prevent Christianity from spreading. Hardest hit is an active Baptist church in Urgench, in northwestern Uzbekistan, which was stripped of its registered status and became "illegal." Secret police, knows as the NSS, questioned at least two Baptists, beating one up, and threatened both Christians with imprisonment "for years" to come.

—RELIGION TODAY

F. Bangladesh

Christian Evangelist Stabbed to Death in Bangladesh by Muslims (6/20/03)

A Christian evangelist became Bangladesh's first martyr in modern times following attack by at least seven Muslim extremists armed with knives. Just after midnight, early in the morning of April 24, [as] Hridoy Roy...approached his house, seven or eight people attacked him, stabbing him seven times. He died instantly. Hridoy Roy was a Bangladeshi evangelist....In Islamic law (Shari'ah) conversion from Islam to another faith (apostasy) is punishable by death. This is a deep-seated tradition among Muslims; and those who do convert, if not killed, are often subject to beatings and having their possessions and family taken away from them.

—RELIGION TODAY

Pastor Beheaded in Bangladesh (6/3/05)

Sources have confirmed the murder by beheading on March 8 of Dulal Sarkar, a lay pastor and evangelist in Bangladesh. Sarkar worked with the Bangladesh Free Baptist Church in Jalalpur village as an evangelist and church planter. On the night of March 8 as he returned home, he was attacked and killed by Muslim extremists. His wife, Aruna, immediately filed a case against the killers, and three suspects were arrested. However, militants are now threatening Aruna and her children. The beheading is the second in the space of a year. Dr. Abdul Gani, a respected Christian leader, was decapitated by a gang of assailants in September 2004.

—RELIGION TODAY

G. Afghanistan

Empty Kabul Church Reflects Fear of Islam (3/29/02)

Once back before the 1979 Soviet invasion of Afghanistan, the Community Christian Church of Kabul was filled with worshipers, mostly foreigners. Since then, war and Kabul's capture by the...Islamic Taliban have made it impossible for Christians to gather in the sanctuary, reports the Boston Daily Globe. A Baptist missionary, living for 33 years in that country, advised, "Everyone is still wary of how services will be received." During the Taliban era, Christianity was banned outright; those accused of promoting it were threatened with execution.

—RELIGION TODAY

III. African Countries:

A. Nigeria

Nigerian Muslims Threaten Christian Nurses Over Worship Services at Hospital (3/15/02)

Muslim militants have threatened to kill Christian nurses unless they stop conducting worship services at a hospital. The nurses work at the Federal Medical Center in the town of Keffi, located in the central state of Nasarawa....An undated letter received recently by hospital management and the hospital's chapter of the Fellowship of Christian Nurses (FCN) said: "We are making it abundantly clear that our thirst for your heads/blood is mounting daily if you continue with your worship services in the hospital unabated."..."How can they ban us from praying or worshiping here," FCN secretary Christiana Shiaki asked, "when the Muslims have two mosques built with public funds for them here in the hospital?"

—RELIGION TODAY

Muslims Massacre Nigerian Christians (9/27/02)

Two months after Muslim militants killed a pastor and 48 members of his church, fresh religious violence has erupted in Yelwa town in the central state of Plateau. The Muslim-Christian clash last month has resulted in the deaths of at least 350 people, Compass Direct reported.

—charismanow.com

Muslim Violence Against Christians in Nigeria (6/20/03)

Continued religious violence in two areas of Nigeria has resulted in several churches being vandalized, as well as a death in an area where such turmoil had been less common.

On November 30, in Ilorin, the capital of Kwara State, suspected Muslim youth vandalized four churches, destroying and stealing church property and vehicles. In the southern city of Osogbo, a group of around 500 Islamic militants conducted raids throughout the town on November 29.

After vandalizing 15 Christian places of prayer, they killed the 24-year-old son of a...pastor, strangling him and then dragging his lifeless body for several kilometers. They then went on to another area of the city where they set fire to other church buildings.

...Religious clashes such as these have resulted in the death of hundreds of people in Nigeria in the past several months.

—*RELIGION TODAY*

Muslims Assault, Kill Christians in Nigeria (5/21/04)

Christians in the Plateau State have been killed and forced from their land by extremist Islamic militants. According to Christian Solidarity Worldwide (CSW), the attacks [in June] in the area surrounding Jos left...four killed and twenty injured....

Several churches were burned, shops and homes were looted, and properties by Christians were destroyed in Yelwa Shendam. The Christians were also chased out of town and forced to take refuge in Jos.

In a separate incident in Wase, believers were attacked and killed, and church buildings destroyed, along with farmland and crops. Christians in the area were forced to flee....Sporadic attacks have also been reported in Berakin Ladi, Vom and Miango, leaving several dead in each attack....

"We are facing a new Muslim onslaught,"...Ben Kwashi of Jos said. "Terror has been released on the majority [of the] Christian population of the Plateau."

—CNS

Jihad in Nigeria (7/16/04)

ABUJA, Nigeria (VOM News)—For several years now, radical Muslims in northern and central Nigeria have been carrying out a "holy" war, or jihad, against Christians....

The attackers, mostly Fulani Muslims, use guns and machetes as their weapons of destruction. They make no distinction between men, women and children—who will not only carry the physical scars for the rest of their lives, but the emotional ones as well....

Hundreds have been killed in Christian villages throughout the state. Homes have been destroyed as the attacks against Christians have intensified.

—*RELIGION TODAY*

Muslims in Nigeria Burn Ten Churches (12/3/04)

Muslim fanatics burned down 10 Christian churches in the town of Makarfi in the northern state of Kaduna, Nigeria [April 10]. Claims that a mentally retarded Christian teenager desecrated the Quran... apparently incited the attack. Although officials initially reported no casualties in the incident, eyewitnesses saw trucks piled with bodies of dead Christians from Makarfi being taken away for burial by police in nearby Kaduna....At a press conference...leaders of the Kaduna chapter of the Christian Association of Nigeria (CAN) confirmed the killings in Makarfi. "It is our conclusion that Muslim leaders are deliberately using fanatics in the name of Islam to engage in periodic attacks on Christians with the sole aim to intimidate, terrorize and force Christians into submission and to denounce their faith," CAN Vice-Chairman Dr. Sam Kjuiyat said.

—*RELIGION TODAY*

Christian Witness Murdered in Nigeria (2/25/05)

Muslim students recently killed a Christian college student after opposition to evangelism broke out on the campuses of two universities [in Nigeria]. Sunday Nache Achi, a fourth-year architectural student at Abubakar Tafawa Balewa University...was strangled to death..., and his body was abandoned next to a mosque, Compass Direct reported.

...University officials had earlier expelled students Abraham Adamu Misal, Hannatu Haruna Alkali and Habakkuk Solomon for distributing a Christian leaflet that compared the teachings of Jesus with Islam.

—charismanow.com

Nigerian Muslims Continue Assaults on Christians (4/22/05)

Muslim militants pronounced a death sentence on five Christian students expelled from colleges in November for conducting an evangelistic outreach. The families of two of the students...were attacked on January 26, when militants went to their family homes in the state of Gombe,...Compass Direct reported....

Authorities of Abubakar Tafawa Balewa University (ATBU) and the Federal Polytechnic in Bauchi expelled...[them] for sharing the Gospel with Muslim students. According to officials of the two schools, Muslims in the schools complained that the Christian students blasphemed the prophet Muhammad.

Sunday Nache Achi, a student and president of the campus chapter of the Evangelical Church of West Africa students' ministry at ATBU, was murdered over the incident on December 8. He was not part of the group of Christian students that conducted the gospel outreach.

—charismanow.com

Nigerian Muslims Slaughter Christian Countrymen (5/20/05)

Muslim militants recently attacked a Christian community, killing 36 people and displacing about 3,000 others. The attack occurred...in Demsa village, located in the African nation's northern region of Adamawa State, Compass Direct reported.

The surviving Christians have taken refuge in Mayolope village in the neighboring state of Taraba. While visiting the displaced Christians...the Rev. Jolly Nyame, governor of the state of Taraba, expressed sadness over the attacks and said the country could progress only through peaceful coexistence....

Nyame added that the Nigerian government needs to check the activities of Muslim militants, who have provoked crises in different parts of the country.

—charismanow.com

B. Kenya

Muslim Tensions Rise and Churches Burn in Kenya (8/1/03)

On June 13, Muslims rioting over the arrest of one of their clerics torched five churches in Bura, Tana River district, in Kenya. Of great concern to Christians in Kenya is the fact that no one has been charged over the burning of the churches. Christian leaders are still waiting to see if the arsonists will receive justice or impunity. As impunity equals permission, this is a serious issue of national significance at a time when Muslim tensions are rising to boiling point.

—*RELIGION TODAY*

C. Senegal

Muslim Mob Storms Senegal Church; Forces Closure (9/27/02)

A local Muslim politician at the head of a mob of young men stormed a church in Dakar on May 23. Insulting and assaulting Christian worshipers, the youths, armed with knives and stones, drove them out and occupied the building. The church, which has only recently opened, first encountered opposition from the local politician when it met with officials to receive formal approval before beginning to hold services.

Having failed to prevent Christians from establishing the church, local conservative Muslims took the law into their own hands and decided to assault the church, claiming that Christians were making too much noise during services and disturbing the local community....

The incident is the latest in a series of several attacks upon Christians and their churches that have taken place in different parts of the country in recent years. Church leaders fear the incidents may be part of a concerted campaign to put pressure on Christians by Islamic extremist factions who want to make Senegal an exclusively Islamic country. Tensions were heightened for Christians and other non-Muslims in the country two years ago when the president announced that "Senegal will be 100 percent Muslim in three years."

—RELIGION TODAY

D. Somalia

Islamists Target Christians (2/13/04)

Several Christians and Westerners have recently been killed in violent attacks on Christian workers in Somalia while a Christian delegation attempts to make itself heard at Somali peace talks. During 2003 several cases of violent attacks against Christians and Westerners took place in Somalia as part of a new wave of persecution....

The attacks appear to be deliberately anti-Christian and anti-Western. In February 2003 a radical Somali Islamist group, Kulanka Culimada, based in Mogadishu, issued a press release in which they called for all Somali Christians to be treated as apostates from Islam who ought to be killed. This was in response to a bold move by the tiny persecuted Christian community in Somalia that had sent several delegates to peace talks currently being held in Nairobi (initiated in 2002) to demand the right of freedom of religion and assembly, political representation and free movement. The Christian representatives were shouted down by Muslim delegates who insisted Somalia had no Christians and who declared Islam to be the official religion of Somalia. This seems to mirror prejudices widely held by Muslim Somalis which justify violence against Christians, both indigenous and expatriate.

—ASSIST News Service

EDITOR'S COMMENTS: Are we getting the picture yet?

Chapter Seven

Muslim Activities Around the World

I. Palestinians Show Strong Support for Suicide Bombings

A. Palestinian Families Obeying "a Holy Duty" to Kill (8/2/02)

GAZA CITY, Gaza Strip—A mother lovingly dresses her 12-year-old son in the homemade costume of a suicide bomber, complete with small kaffiyeh, a belt of electrical tape and fake explosives made of plywood.

"I encourage him, and he should do this," said the woman, the mother of six. "...Palestinian women must have more and more children till we liberate our land. This is a holy duty for all Palestinian people."

Her son, Abu Ali, joyfully marched in a mask on the day commemorating the Nakba, or "catastrophe," as Palestinians call the day of Israel's founding in 1948.

"I hope to be a martyr," he said. "I hope when I get to 14 or 15 to explode myself."

The suicide bomber thrives on a culture of fatalism, nurtured in a landscape of poverty and hopelessness, and popularized by a Palestinian government whose policies have demonized Israel.

Millions of Palestinians are encouraged to stay in squalid refugee camps, a rebuke to the Jewish state's existence. Textbooks don't even show Israel on the map.

During the current intifada, or uprising, against Israel's military and economic dominance, the martyr has become the ultimate weapon....

Since January 2000, there have been 119 incidents throughout Israel proper and against Israeli targets in Gaza and the West Bank, Israeli police spokesman Gil Kleiman said.

—*WASHINGTON TIMES*

EDITOR'S COMMENTS: When such wicked behavior is defined as "a holy duty," it is a sad commentary on their religion, their politics and whatever else motivates them!

B. West Bank Celebrates "Martyrdom" of Girl Suicide Bomber (8/16/02)

BEIT FAJAR, West Bank (AFP)—Residents of the village of Beit Fajar are braving the curfew to visit Khalil Takatka, to congratulate him on the "martyrdom" of his 20-year-old daughter, Andaleeb, who blew herself to pieces in a suicide attack in Jerusalem, killing six other people.

Women wearing the traditional clothes of the Bethlehem region, embroidered in black and red, defied Israeli troops to make their way in little groups to Takatka's home, singing patriotic songs.

"We want to congratulate the family of the young Andaleeb and remember her heroism," said one of the women.

"It is your celebration, Andaleeb," said another, adding that the day of the suicide attack should be considered "her wedding day."

Andaleeb's mother, Aziza, recounted how a few hours before the attack her daughter "bought sweets and candies and distributed them to the neighbors telling them, 'You will soon hear good news.'"

Pictures of the young girl and Palestinian flags adorn the walls of the village, which is located south of Bethlehem and has 12,000 inhabitants. Patriotic songs are broadcast from speakers.

Aziza Takatka said she was "sad" at the death of her daughter but stressed that she also felt "proud and joyful."...

On the walls of her little cement house,...the Al-Aqsa Martyrs Brigades, linked to Arafat's Fatah party, and the Islamic movement Hamas have hung streamers "congratulating" the Palestinian people

86

for the "martyrdom of Andaleeb."...

In front of Andaleeb's house, three girls aged five to nine were waiting. When asked, "What do you want to do?" one of them replied, "We wish to die in martyr operations."

C. Thousands in Gaza Celebrate Jerusalem Attack (9/13/02)

GAZA—About 10,000 Palestinians handed out sweets, sang songs and chanted anti-Israeli slogans as they marched through Gaza City [July 31] to celebrate the bombing that killed seven people at Jerusalem's Hebrew University.

—NEW ZEALAND HERALD

D. Arab Archbishop Praises Suicide Bombers (2/14/03)

A Palestinian archbishop is urging Arab Christians to join forces with Islam and take part in suicide attacks against Israel, reports ASSIST News Service.

Greek Orthodox Archbishop Attallah Hanna, former spokesman of the Orthodox Church of Jerusalem and the Holy Land, called for the creation of an Islamic-Christian union that would foil the "American offensive" against Iraq and "release Palestine from the river to the sea."

"The suicide bombers who carry out their activities in the name of religion are national [Islamic] heroes, and we're proud of them," he said on the Internet website of the militant group Hamas....

The 37-year-old Archbishop Hanna also called on Arab and Palestinian Christians to join the struggle against the occupation by employing "any means at their disposal."

E. Palestinian Soccer Tournament Honors Suicide Bomber (2/28/03)

JERUSALEM (CNSNews.com)—Seven Palestinian sports teams, all named after Palestinians killed in violence against Israel, participated in the opening of a soccer tournament in honor of the suicide bomber who blew himself up in a hotel in Netanya on the eve of Passover last year, according to a newspaper report on [January 21].

F. Palestinians Honor Iraqi Suicide Bomber (5/9/03)

JERUSALEM (CNSNews.com)—Palestinians have honored the first suicide bomber to attack allied troops in Iraq by naming the central square of the Jenin refugee camp after him, Jenin residents confirmed on [April 1].

EDITOR'S COMMENTS: On April Fool's Day, no less!

G. Muslim Camps Train Children to Kill, Documentary Says (1/16/04)

NASHVILLE, Tenn. (BP)—Extremist Islamic camps in the Middle East train more than 10,000 Arab children each year how to commit suicide bombings, perpetrate other acts of violence and develop hatred toward Jews, according to The New Barbarians, a documentary produced by filmmaker, Caryl Matrisciana....

The documentary, released earlier this year, also contends that a significant number of the 1.6 million Muslims in the United States financially support the Middle Eastern camps.

Matrisciana, who has more than 20 years' experience as a filmmaker, produced The New Barbarians by compiling footage from Arab television, news reports and other documentaries. This footage shows the graphic aftermath of terrorist bombings and details how Islamic camps are training Arab children as young as 5 years old to use machine guns, slit human throats, hijack cars and strap explosives to themselves, Matrisciana told Baptist Press.

In one scene, an Arab reporter asks a 5-year-old Muslim boy, "Do you want to be a martyr?"

The boy answers, "Yes."

"Why?" probes the reporter.

"To kill the Jews," the boy replies.

H. Young Mother Blows Herself Up at Gaza Border (3/26/04)

EREZ CROSSING, Gaza—A Palestinian blew herself up [January 14] at the Israel-Gaza border. The attack killed three Israeli soldiers and a private security guard and signaled a new tactic by Hamas terrorists, who had never before used a female suicide bomber.

Hamas spiritual leader Ahmed Yassin said the use of a woman was unique for the Islamic group, but holy war "is an obligation of all Muslims, men and women."

...Some Palestinians expressed anger at the suicide bombing because it could cost them their jobs.

The army said four of the seven people wounded in the attack were Palestinians.

Violence over the past 39 months has killed 2,618 Palestinians and 909 Israelis.

...Reem Raiyshi, 22, told soldiers she would set off a metal detector because she had an implant to repair a broken leg. She was taken for a security search to a special room, where she set off the bomb, said Major Sharon Feingold, a military spokeswoman.

...Though other militant groups have used women to carry out bombings, Hamas had not....

In a video made before the bombing, Raiyshi wears the traditional hijab covering for women, she holds an assault rifle and stands before two green Hamas flags. "I always wanted to be the first woman to carry out a martyr attack, where parts of my body can fly all over. That is the only wish I can ask God for," she says.

Raiyshi had a daughter, Doha, 18 months, and a son, Obedia, 3.

—USA TODAY

EDITOR'S COMMENTS: From every angle of reasoned and civilized thinking, it is totally inconceivable that any human being could even contemplate such a barbaric—in fact, insane—act.

Noticeably, this young Arab and Islamic mother attributed her criminal suicide to "God." Who in his or her right mind would yield to and serve a "god" who thus instructs and motivates its faithful?

I. Atoning for Misdeeds With "Martyrdom" (3/26/04)

JERUSALEM—A Palestinian mother of two small children, who killed four Israelis by blowing herself up at a border crossing [January 14], carried out the suicide bombing to atone for having committed adultery.

The attack marked the first time the militant group Hamas had used a female bomber, part of an evolving belief that women who are disgraced by sexual activity outside marriage can "purify themselves by becoming martyrs," Israeli security officials said.

The officials, who closely monitor the evolving ideology of the Islamic militant organization, spoke to reporters in the wake of the attack by 22-year-old Reem Raiyshi.

Raiyshi left her 18-month-old daughter, Doha, and her 3-year-old son, Obedia, and blew herself up at the Erez crossing between the Gaza Strip and Israel, killing three soldiers and a private Israeli security guard....

Hamas spiritual leader Sheik Ahmed Yassin told reporters in the Gaza Strip on January 19 that the militant group would look to women to step up and fulfill their "obligations."

—WASHINGTON TIMES

II. They Are Engaged in a Terror War

A. Al Qaida Prepares Attacks, Kidnappings Against "Zionists" and Americans (2/28/03)

(ASSIST News)—The al-Qaida network that claimed the September 11 suicide attacks against the United States has ordered its members to abduct "Zionists" and carry out suicide bombings at embassies and airports around the world, reports said Tuesday, January 21. In a letter that appeared on a Web site identified with al-Qaida leader Osama bin Laden, the group called on members to rid the world of "nonbelievers," the International Christian Embassy Jerusalem (ICEJ) News Service reported. "Attempts must be made to abduct...one or two Americans or Zionists. Focus on abducting journalists or famous people in order to pressure [the US or Israel]," al-Qaida was quoted as telling its supporters. It ordered members to target embassies all over the world that belong to "enemies," suggesting missile attacks against the buildings as "some of the embassies are located in areas suitable for missile attacks." Al-Qaida gives several examples of different ways to carry out attacks, including car bombs detonated by remote control, or suicide bombers who detonate simultaneously to create a "greater effect."

B. Indonesia Accuses Muslim Cleric of Treason (6/20/03)

Indonesian prosecutors charged Muslim cleric Abu Bakar Bashir with treason for leading the Jemaah Islamiyah terror network and for authorizing church bombings that killed 19 people. The group has been linked to al-Qaeda. Bashir, 64, also is accused of plotting to blow up U.S. targets in Singapore....He is accused of involvement in bombings of churches throughout Indonesia around Christmas 2000.

—*USA TODAY*

C. Saudis Exporting Hateful Form of Islam (1/16/04)

WASHINGTON (BP)—Saudi Arabia exports an intolerant, violence-producing form of Islam to other countries, including the United States, witnesses told the U.S. Commission on International Religious Freedom.

The royal family that rules Saudi Arabia is wedded to an extremist strain of Islam known as Wahhabism that controls the leaders of the country's 71,000 mosques, as well as the educational system, the panel was told. Despite a recent denial by the Saudi government, this form of Islam is being exported to schools in other countries with Saudi funds, the witnesses said.

"Not only has the state embraced the hard-liners, the hard-liners are the state," said Mai Yamani, a Saudi national who works in London as an expert on her native country. "Saudi Arabia is guilty of propagating intolerance" globally, she said....

This spreading of hate is happening in schools "in the United States as well," [Martin] Indyk [a Middle East expert and former ambassador to Israel] said. "We should not be surprised by that."

D. Satellite Television Station Airs Hatred of U.S. Globally (12/3/04)

Every evening about ten million people across the world are tuning in to Al-Manar television, a satellite channel that lauds suicide bombers, accuses the United States of crimes against humanity and shows the Statue of Liberty as a gory, knife-wielding figure dripping blood.

They also hear a clear and violent call to arms against U.S. troops in Iraq and Israeli forces.

One video juxtaposes U.S. footage of soldiers with gory corpses and ends with a suicide bomber's belt exploding, all set to these lyrics:

"Down with the mother of terrorism. America threatens in vain an occupying army of invaders. Nothing remains but rifles and suicide bombers."

The State Department said it has long viewed Al-Manar as being funded and run by Hezbollah, a U.S.-designated terrorist organization funded by Iran, but based in Lebanon.

"We've always been deeply troubled by Al-Manar's programming and content, its anti-Semitic bias, incitement to violence, including support for insurrection in Iraq and terrorist actions against both the U.S. and Israel," said State Department spokesman Gregg Sullivan....

Second only to Al-Jazeera in popularity in the West Bank and Gaza Strip, Al-Manar has correspondents in Belgium, France, Iraq, Kosovo, Kuwait, Morocco, the Palestinian territories, Russia, Sweden, Turkey, Syria and the United States, said Avi Jorisch, who spent two years researching the station....

The television station also features short clips with photographs of suicide bombers popping up in Hollywood-type stars, as simulated bomb blasts occur behind them.

One short film features the September 11 attacks on the World Trade Center towers and asks: "Why are some ruling out an American or Zionist as the perpetrator?" and "Why would Arabs and Muslims feel guilty about a crime that has not been proven to have been committed by them?"

—WASHINGTON TIMES

E. Islamic Groups Planning Worldwide Anti-U.S. Protests (8/12/05)

Radical Islamic groups are pressing ahead with plans for worldwide anti-U.S. protests....A demonstration in Indonesia...indicated the level of anger directed toward America over Koran abuse allegations.

"Destroy America and its allies," Indonesian extremist leader Muhammad Iqbal told a rally outside the U.S. Embassy in Jakarta, using a public address system to address the crowd. "Kill those who desecrate Islam."

An estimated 7,000 Muslims protested in the Indonesian capital, a gathering that drew several dozen Islamic organizations, including the mainstream "moderate" groups Nahdlatul Ulama and Muhammadiyah, each of which claims millions of members.

—CNSNews.com

F. Muslim Leaders Condemn London Attacks but Still Say Some Bombings Justified (9/9/05)

Muslim leaders and scholars condemned the London bombings...but stopped short of criticizing all suicide attacks. Some of them said that bombers targeting occupying forces are sometimes justified.

The 22 imams and scholars, meeting at London's largest mosque, said in a joint statement that the perpetrators of the subway blasts had violated the Quran by killing innocent civilians and no one should consider them martyrs.

In a later news conference the conferences were repeatedly asked if they also condemn suicide bombings in countries such as Iraq and Israel.

"There should be a clear distinction between the suicide bombing of those who are trying to defend themselves from occupiers, which is something different from those who kill civilians, which is a big crime," said Sayed Mohammed Musawi, the head of the World Islamic League in London.

The media in the West are mixing the difference between these two, and the result is that some of our Muslim youth are becoming more frustrated."...

The statement also said that racism, unemployment and economic deprivation that Muslims face in poor sections of cities such as Leeds—where three of the suspected bombers lived—"may be alienating some of our children and driving them toward the path of anger and desperation" in ways that are prohibited by Islam.

—*NASHVILLE TENNESSEAN*

EDITOR'S COMMENTS: Double-talk! Hedging on such clear-cut issues of right and wrong, as well as life and death, is mealy-mouthed double-talk!

III. The Religious Climate Where Islam Holds Sway

A. It Is an Antagonistic Environment for Spreading the Gospel

1. Evangelism of Muslims Is Not a "Hate Crime" (3/14/03)

[Propagating] the Gospel in most Muslim nations is a criminal act.

Trying to change someone's religion is depicted as hateful. Social ministry is seen as a mere smoke screen. From ignorance, some say Muslims do not need converting because Christians and Muslims believe in and worship the same God (2/03 *C. Today*). A University of Chicago Divinity School professor years ago said Christians should not try to convert pious Muslims to Christianity. He said: "Christianity is the authentic form of religion for us in our culture, but Islam is the authentic form of religion for them in theirs." But differences between the two are more than merely cultural, and it's not a "hate crime" to point one to the One who has the true Gospel.

—CALVARY CONTENDER

2. Missionaries' Perils Grow As Muslim, Hindu Zealots Turn More Violent (3/14/03)

As...Christian emissaries have spread throughout the Muslim world, their presence has increasingly proved to be a lightning rod for anti-American sentiment while provoking the anger of native Christian sects and Islamic clerics....

The negative reaction is not limited to Muslim countries but has been seen in Hindu-dominated nations such as India....

"With the rise of religious politics, whether they are Muslim or Hindu, missionaries come into the cross hairs of Muslim and Hindu fundamentalists," said Bernard Haykel, an assistant professor of Middle Eastern studies and history at New York University. "Certainly as the Arab and Muslim world has become more radicalized Islamically, people have become more aware of missionaries and more irritated by them."...

...Missionaries [have] found that proselytizing to Muslims was a dangerous business. Under Muslim law, conversion from Islam is punishable by death.

—COLUMBUS [Ohio] *DISPATCH*

B. Christian/Muslim Tension in Nigeria

1. Nigerian Christian Governor Urged to Convert to Islam (5/24/02)

Impressed by his support for Muslims in Adamawa State, North East Nigeria, the Muslim community has urged the state governor, Boni Haruna, who is a Christian, to convert to Islam. The acting chairman of the Adamawa Muslim Council, Yusuf Aliyu, made the call during a...Muslim festival...visit to the governor, reports Lekan Otufodunrin of Nigeria Online Christian News Service, Lagos.

"Accept Islam and come back home, as it is the religion of your grandfather," the Muslim council chairman stated. "In fact, we are here to receive you back into our faith."

The governor, according to the council, has won the support and confidence of the Muslim population in the state for his unbiased treatment of citizens, irrespective of their faith....

...Nigeria is evenly divided among Christians and Muslims. Christians dominate the South, while Muslims are in the majority in the North.

—RELIGION TODAY

2. Islamic Law Threatens Nigeria (5/24/02)

"The enforcement of extreme 'sharia' Islam law violates all human rights, especially religious freedom, and destabilizes this already fragile country," advised Dr. Paul Marshall, in a major report released by Freedom House's Center for Religious Freedom. "If left unchecked, sharia's further spread...could transform Nigeria...into a center of radical Islamism...with lawlessness and terror, like Afghanistan under the Taliban."

In the report, Marshall said the "effect on human rights" is even more "profound and far wider" than the harsh, inhumane, physically disabling punishments, and he listed four new rules that not only undermine such rights but violate Nigeria's constitution.

Having only just begun on the road to democracy, Nigeria is struggling, and reports are that the growth of Islamic extremism is being supported by foreign radical Islamic regimes such as Sudan and Saudi Arabia.

—RELIGION TODAY

3. Nigerian Citizens Speak Out Against Islamic Law (1/3/03)

Political and religious leaders in Nigeria continue an intense debate over the implementation of Sharia, or Islamic law, by 12 of the country's 36 states. Some Muslim politicians appear to agree with Christian leaders that the imposition of Sharia is undemocratic. Bola

Ahmed Tinubu, governor of the state of Lagos, where 6 of 10 residents are Christians, told a gathering of journalists and religious leaders that members of the Muslim community have been pressuring him to introduce the Islamic legal code. He rebuffed the attempt. Tinubu, a Muslim, expressed sadness that some politicians are deliberately dismantling the Nigerian state. "The nation's crisis can be traced to the desperation of people who want to gain power," he said. In the three years since states introduced Sharia, over 100,000 Nigerians have suffered displacement and more than 3,000 have died in riots.

—RELIGION TODAY

4. Islamic Intolerance Stirs Trouble (4/25/03)

(Compass)—Religious tension between Muslims and Christians in Nigeria has moved to yet another social arena: education. Last month, Muslim extremists attacked Christian mission schools in the city of Ibadan, injuring hundreds of students and teachers. The violence spread across the city, bringing commercial activities to a standstill for hours before police intervened to restore order. The National Council of Muslim Youth Organizations of Nigeria organized the attacks, saying in a press statement that the objective was to press administrators to require female students to wear the Hijap, a Muslim head covering. Police arrested 51 of the assailants. In another development, Muslim teachers in Ondo state rejected calls by churches to return to them all Christian mission schools seized without compensation in 1977 by the government. The teachers argued that returning the confiscated schools would amount to "privatization and commercialization of education."

C. Results of Islamic Law

1. Death by Stoning Highlights Risks to Christians Under Islam (4/12/02)

A Sudanese court has sentenced a Christian woman to death by stoning for alleged adultery, and religious freedom campaigners say the case helps explain why Christian minorities in many Muslim societies oppose the imposition of Islamic law.

New York-based Human Rights Watch has written to Sudan's president to appeal for the "cruel and inhuman" sentence to be lifted against 18-year-old Abok Alfa Akok, who was sentenced to death last

December by a criminal court in southwestern Sudan....

An exiled Iranian opposition group, the National Council of Resistance (NCRI), claims that since the 1979 Islamic revolution, "hundreds of women of various ages have been and continue to be stoned to death throughout Iran."...

More than two million people are believed to have died during an 18-year civil war between the Islamic regime in Khartoum and the mostly animist and Christian South.

The US Congress has defined the conflict as a "genocidal war," and human rights groups have recorded the widespread enslavement.

—*RELIGION TODAY*

2. Sudan Jihad Forces Islam on Christians (7/5/02)

Sudan's militant Muslim regime is slaughtering Christians who refuse to convert to Islam, according to the head of an aid group who recently returned from the African nation.

The forced conversions are just one aspect of the Khartoum government's self-declared jihad on the mostly Christian and animist South, Dennis Bennett, executive director of Seattle-based Servant's Heart told WorldNetDaily.

Villagers in several areas of the northeast Upper Nile region say that when women are captured by government forces, they are asked, "Are you Christian or Muslim?"

Women who answer "Muslim" are set free, but typically soldiers gang-rape those who answer "Christian," [inflict other atrocities] and leave them to die as an example for others....

Backed by Muslim clerics, the National Islamic Front regime in the Arab and Muslim North declared a jihad, or holy war, on the South in 1989. Since 1983, an estimated 2 million people have died from war and related famine....

Sudan's holy war against the South was reaffirmed in October by First Vice President Ali Osman Taha.

"The jihad is our way, and we will not abandon it and will keep its banner high," he said to a brigade of mujahedin fighters heading for the war front, according to Sudan's official SUNA news agency....

The U.S. House of Representatives adopted a resolution finding that Khartoum is "systematically committing genocide."...

...Sudan's military continues to decorate and promote known war criminals such as Commander Taib Musba, who in the mid-1980s killed an estimated 15,000 unarmed, civilian, ethnic Uduk Christians.

In 1986, Musba entered the Uduk tribal capital of Chali and declared to its Christians: "You are all going to convert from Christianity to Islam today, because here is what's going to happen to you if you don't."

Musba then killed five church leaders in front of the gathered villagers. When they refused to convert, he began killing unarmed men, women and children. Some were herded at gunpoint into a hut, then run over by a 50-ton, Soviet-made tank.

He also herded groups of about a dozen people into a hut, where he asked the first person, "Do you renounce Jesus Christ?" Anyone who refused was killed by a three-inch nail driven into the top of the head....

Forced starvation is one of the primary tools of the Khartoum regime, [Bennett] says. When government forces attack a Christian village, they kill everyone they catch, but those who flee lose everything necessary for survival.

"The government comes in and burns the crops, burns grain stored if there was any excess, burns houses down," Bennett said. "Now you have only the clothes on your back—no tools, no cooking pots, no buckets for water—and you have to run two days through the bush in 115-degree temperatures in order to escape."

—worldnetdaily.com

3. "Pleasure Marriages" Regain Popularity in Iraq (7/29/05)

In the days when it could land him in jail, Rahim Al-Zaidi would whisper details of his muta'a only to his closest confidants and the occasional cousin. Never his wife.

Al-Zaidi hopes soon to finalize his third muta'a, or "pleasure marriage," with a green-eyed neighbor. This time he talks about it openly and with obvious relish. Even so, he says, he probably still won't tell his wife.

The 1,400-year-old practice of muta'a—"ecstasy" in Arabic—is as old as Islam itself. It was permitted by the prophet Mohammed as a way to ensure a respectable means of income for widowed women.

Pleasure marriages were outlawed under Saddam Hussein but have begun to flourish again...."Under Saddam, we were very scared," says Al-Zaidi, 39, a lawyer from Sadr City, a sprawling Shiite neighborhood in eastern Baghdad. "They would punish people. Now, all my friends are doing it."

A turbaned Shiite cleric who issues wedding permits from a street-side counter in Sadr City says he encourages permanent marriages but gives the okay for pleasure marriages when there are "special reasons."

—*USA TODAY*

IV. The Climate in Other Non-Muslim Countries

A. Using Hate-Speech Laws for Advantage

1. Muslim-Christian Clash Looms Over Islamic Teachings (8/16/02)

An Australian Muslim organization, seizing on controversial new hate legislation, has filed a complaint against a Christian group it accuses of vilifying Islam. The Christians say all they did was quote from Islamic scriptures, but the Muslims claim the seminar incited "fear and hatred" against Muslims.

—CNSNews.com

2. Australian Pastor Faces Hate-Speech Violation (5/7/04)

Pacific Rim Bureau—God and Allah are not the same, an Australian pastor has told a tribunal where he faces complaints of vilifying Islam.

Pastor Daniel Scot, a scholar in Islam who fled his native Pakistan 17 years ago amid threats of retribution for "blasphemy," said that his studying of the Bible and the Quran led him to the conclusion that the God of the Bible and Allah of the Quran were different in practice, behavior and other attributes.

Scot and another pastor, Danny Nalliah, have been appearing before an administrative tribunal in the state of Victoria, after Muslims brought a complaint against them under controversial new hate laws.

99

Nalliah's organization...organized a seminar on Islam for Christians in March 2002, and Scot was the guest speaker. Three Muslim converts who attended the meeting at the request of the Islamic Council of Victoria (ICV) said the seminar had incited fear of, and hatred for, Muslims....

If the judge upholds the complaint, he may order Scot and Nalliah to apologize, pay compensation or take other steps. The specific complaint faced by the two does not carry criminal penalties.

—CNSNews.com

3. Australian Pastors Found Guilty of Vilifying Islam (1/14/05)

Christians in Australia are pondering the implication of an explosive ruling handed down [December 17] by a legal tribunal, which found that two Christian pastors had vilified Islam.

Immediate reactions ranged from an evangelical commentator's view that the decision spelled "the beginning of the end of freedom of speech in Australia" to that of a liberal church denomination which said it sent a welcome message to "Christian extremist groups."

One of the pastors at the center of the dispute said...it would galvanize Christians and other Australians who cared about free speech.

Pastors Danny Nalliah and Daniel Scot were found to have breached a section of the state of Victoria's controversial hate law, which says a person must not incite "hatred against, serious contempt for or revulsion or severe ridicule of" another person or group on the basis of religious belief or activity.

The complaint arose from a seminar on Islam run for Christians by Nalliah's evangelical Catch the Fire Ministries in Melbourne in 2002.

Three Muslims attended on behalf of the Islamic Council of Victoria and subsequently submitted a complaint under the state's Racial and Religious Tolerance Act....

The law provides for exemptions in cases where the offending action was taken "reasonably and in good faith...for any genuine academic, artistic, religious or scientific purpose" or in the public interest.

But [tribunal judge Michael] Higgins found that the exemptions did not apply in the case before him.

"I find that Pastor Scot's conduct was not engaged in reasonably and in good faith for any genuine religious purpose or any purpose that is in the public interest."

Scot, a Pakistan-born scholar of Islam, was the main speaker at the seminar. He and Nalliah argued throughout the case that they had merely informed Christians attending the seminar about Islam and its teachings, based on the religion's own texts.

The judge disagreed.

"Pastor Scot, throughout the seminar, made fun of Muslim beliefs and conduct," [the judge] said in the summary....

Higgins referred to some of Scot's statements, including the view that the Koran "promotes violence, killing and looting"; that Muslims are liars; that Allah is not merciful and a thief's hand is cut off for stealing; and that Muslims intend to take over Australia and declare it an Islamic nation....

Higgins said Nalliah suggested that Muslims were "seeking to take over Australia."

"Viewed objectively and in their totality, these statements are likely to incite a feeling of hatred towards Muslims."

—CNSNews.com

4. 82-Year-Old Priest Fined for Speaking Against Islam (2/27/04)

A French priest has been found guilty of "provoking discrimination, hatred or violence" for comments he made critical of the Quran, Islam's holy book.

Philippe Sulmont, 82, was fined $990 for expressing his thoughts in a letter to his parishioners..., Agence France-Presse reported.

"The Asiatics proliferate and invade our land, bringing with them an ideology that threatens the whole world," he wrote.

"Indeed I would add there is no such thing as 'moderate' Islam. All the populations infected by the Muslim religion are indoctrinated by the Quran—a holy book which is the manual for the extension of the kingdom of the Devil at the expense of the kingdom of Christ."

Sulmont was required to give one euro to the organization that sought his conviction, the League of Human Rights. He also must pay for the judgment to be published in two local newspapers, AFP reported.

—WorldNetDaily

EDITOR'S COMMENTS: When "hate speech" is criminalized, you can fully expect that it will apply to situations just such as this. We must keep an ear to the ground for any and all legislation which could be used to silence our voices.

5. California Muslims Honor Author of Hate-Crimes Resolution (9/10/04)

The Sacramento Valley office of the Council on American-Islamic Relations (CAIR-SV) hosted a reception this week to honor Assembly Member Dr. Judy Chu (D-Monterey Park), the author of Assembly Joint Resolution 64 (AJR64). The reception also honored legislators, government officials, law enforcement authorities, community leaders and organizations that supported the anti-hate crimes resolution. AJR64, which targeted bias-motivated crimes against Arab Americans, Muslim Americans, South Asian Americans and Sikhs, was adopted by the California State Assembly (72-0)....California is the first state in the United States to adopt such a resolution....

"AJR64 is an important statement by California legislators that reflects their commitment to fight hate," said Dr. Hamza ElNakhal of CAIR-SV's executive committee. "Muslim Californians welcome this action by the legislature and are grateful for the support."

—cair-net.org

EDITOR'S COMMENTS: Unless I'm badly fooled, Muslims in America have not had any more "hate" hurled at them than is the norm for all of us. We say again, this so-called "hate crimes" legislation is not good news for anybody. It will get a toehold and will soon be used to silence opposition and to deprive Christians especially of their right to express negative opinions about a lot of things.

6. British Political Leader Arrested for Calling Islam "Wicked" (1/14/05)

The leader of a far-right political party in Britain was arrested [December 14] on suspicion of incitement to racial hatred after he was secretly filmed calling Islam a "vicious, wicked" religion.

British National Party (BNP) leader Nick Griffin was questioned by police in the northern English city of Halifax before being released on bail and told to reappear at a police station next March.

Speaking to reporters after being released, he repeated his view that "there are aspects of that religion which are wicked," and he cited the treatment of women under Islam....

A BBC television documentary on the BNP last July included footage of Griffin making the remarks at a meeting, which was filmed by an undercover journalist who had infiltrated the party.

"This wicked, vicious faith has expanded through a handful of cranky lunatics about 1,300 years ago until it is now sweeping country after country," Griffin said.

He told the meeting that in the Koran "you will find verse after verse after verse which says that you can take any woman you want as long as they are not Muslim women."...

It is not yet illegal in Britain to incite religious hatred, so Griffin instead will face charges of inciting racial hatred.

The British government recently introduced a proposal creating a new criminal offense of inciting "hatred against a group of persons defined by reference to religious belief or lack of religious belief."

Critics say the proposed legislation could be widely abused, preventing people from criticizing another religion or even trying to win converts.

—CNSNews.com

EDITOR'S COMMENTS: The stories above clearly show the direction the "hate speech" paranoia is headed.

7. UK Edges Closer to Outlawing Religious "Hate Speech" (4/22/05)

Controversial anti-hate-speech legislation moved closer to becoming law in Britain on [February 14], and religious and civil groups from across the political spectrum remain bitterly divided over its potential effects.

Despite claims by the Labor government that proposals to outlaw speech inciting religious hatred will simply close existing legal loopholes, opponents from secular and religious groups claim that it will have a chilling effect on free speech.

The legislation would outlaw "words, behavior or material [that] are...likely to be heard or seen by any person in whom they are...likely to stir up racial or religious hatred."...

Some British opponents of the bill have pointed to a situation in Australia, where similar legislation in place in one state has resulted in two Christian pastors being found guilty of vilifying Islam.

—*RELIGION TODAY*

8. Religious Hate-Speech Proposal Appears Doomed in Britain (5/6/05)

The British government is expected to drop a contentious proposal to outlaw religious incitement, having failed to get the legislation through the House of Lords quickly enough to avoid running out of parliamentary time.

...Lawmakers will sit only until [April 8] before parliament is dissolved and the election campaign begins.

As a result, and because of strong opposition in the upper House of Lords, the government is unlikely to push through the religious hate-speech measure, which forms part of a broader crime bill.

The House of Lords will either vote down the entire Serious Organized Crime and Police Bill [April 5], or the government may agree to drop the controversial section in order to get the rest of the legislation passed before parliament dissolves.

—*RELIGION TODAY*

B. Osama Bin Laden Honored by Muslims Abroad

1. Bin Laden Hailed as "Hero" (11/8/02)

LONDON (CNSNews.com)—Attendees at a radical Islamic conference held one year after the September 11 attacks hailed terrorist leader Osama bin Laden as a "hero" and warned of possible suicide bombings in the United States and Britain.

The conference at the Finsbury Park mosque in north London was organized by al-Muhajiroun, a radical group that advocates the worldwide imposition of strict Islamic law.

Wednesday's proceedings were led by al-Muhajiroun leader Sheikh Omar Bakri Mohammed and Abu Hamza al-Masri, who is wanted in Yemen for his alleged connections to the Islamic Army of Aden—the group that claimed responsibility for the bombing of the USS Cole in October 2000.

Before the conference, Bakri denied the event was a "celebration" of the September 11 attacks but admitted the conference included discussion topics such as "The Positive Outcomes of September 11."...

Another radical cleric, Muhammad al-Massari, called the September 11 attacks "legitimate."...

Al-Massari called bin Laden a hero who was "fighting according to his beliefs."

2. Officials Refuse Permission to Name Son Osama Bin Laden (11/8/02)

BERLIN—German authorities have denied a Turkish couple's request to name their newborn son Osama bin Laden, a court spokeswoman said [September 5].

"Osama bin Laden is a great man," the baby's father, Mehmet Cengiz, an unemployed truck driver, told Germany's RTL television. "He's a good man for his people, for my culture."

German laws make it illegal for parents to give their children names that might dishonor them or harm their dignity.
—SOUTH FLORIDA'S SUN-SENTINEL

EDITOR'S COMMENTS: Osama bin Laden is deemed a hero in much of the Islamic world.

C. Muslim Leader Elected to Canadian Civil Liberties Group (9/24/04)

The head of the Canadian Council of American-Islamic Relations (CAIR-CAN) has been elected to the board of directors of the prestigious Canadian Civil Liberties Association (CCLA). CAIR-CAN Chair, Dr. Sheema Khan, joins the CCLA Board for a two-year term.

The CCLA was formed in 1964 and is operated with a volunteer board of directors made up of prominent citizens that include some of Canada's most well-known names in law, journalism, politics, the arts, labor, business and other fields.

—cair-net.org

EDITOR'S COMMENTS: In a post 9-11 world there is an aggressive effort to legitimize and mainstream Islam. The infiltration of the institutions of the North American culture is rapid, and it is purposeful! To the naive and uninformed and for the sake of all of us, we say, Beware!

D. New Pope Promptly Meets With Islamic Leaders (7/15/05)

Muslims in the U.S. hailed Pope Benedict XVI's meeting with Islamic leaders at the Vatican on [April 25], saying they are increasingly confident the new pontiff wants better ties between the world's two largest religions.

The former cardinal Joseph Ratzinger met with Islamic leaders who had attended his installation Mass the day before, promising to work toward building "bridges of friendship" between Catholics and Muslims.

"It is encouraging to note that a meeting with Muslims was one of the first official acts of Pope Benedict XVI," said Ibrahim Hooper, a spokesman for the Washington-based Council on American-Islamic Relations. "We hope that this initial positive step is a sign that he intends to build on Pope John Paul II's legacy of interfaith dialogue and reconciliation."

—cair-net.org

E. London Mayor Defended "Theologian of Terror" (9/9/05)

London mayor Ken Livingstone's previous support of a Muslim cleric who advocates suicide bombings may cause him some embarrassment as he now must speak for the city in the wake of...terrorists bombings.

Livingstone condemned the...attacks as "mass murder" and added that "this was not a terrorist attack against the mighty or the powerful, it was not aimed at presidents or prime ministers, it was aimed at ordinary working-class Londoners."

Yet Livingstone has in the past labeled Sheikh Yusuf Al-Qaradawi a "man of peace" and a "moderate," despite the fact that Al-Qaradawi has supported suicide bombings and the targeting of American allies.

Livingstone invited Al-Qaradawi to London's City hall last year as an honored guest, and the mayor appeared in a video shown at a solidarity conference for the sheikh on February 17 of this year in Doha, Qatar. Livingstone has publicly defended the sheikh against critics in the media and various grass-roots organizations....

Al-Qaradawi is a prominent member of the Muslim Brotherhood, and his fatwas, or theological rulings, are said to influence millions of followers who consider him an authoritative scholar on Islamic issues.

—*RELIGION TODAY*

Chapter Eight
Muslims in America

I. Terrorist Activities in the U.S.

A. Mideast Illegals in U.S. Contributed to 9-11 Attacks (5/10/02)

New U.S. Census Bureau statistics say there may be more than 100,000 illegal aliens of Mideast descent in the United States, a figure that is raising concern among some immigration and terrorism experts.

According to an analysis by the Washington, D.C.-based Center for Immigration Studies, perhaps as many as 115,000 illegal immigrants from various Mideast nations are currently residing in the U.S.

"The findings are especially troubling given the role failures in immigration control played in September's terrorist attacks," said Steven A. Camarota, the center's director of research.

"Not only were at least three of the September 11 hijackers illegal aliens, a number of past terrorists have also been illegal aliens...," Camarota said.

—worldnetdaily.com

B. Al-Qaeda Likely to "Revisit" White House, FBI and CIA Warn (5/7/04)

The al-Qaeda terrorist group still is planning to attack the White House and Congress—targets the group missed on September 11—and a growing extremist Muslim movement is threatening the United States, the directors of the FBI and CIA told Congress on February 24.

"There are strong indications that al-Qaeda will revisit missed targets until they succeed, such as they did with the World Trade Center," FBI Director Robert S. Mueller III told the Senate Select Committee on Intelligence. "And the list of missed targets now includes both the White House as well as the Capitol."

Mr. Mueller said al-Qaeda is seeking to obtain nuclear, chemical and biological weapons for attacks on targets that also include transportation systems, such as subways, bridges in major cities and airliners.

CIA Director George J. Tenet told the committee that al-Qaeda has been weakened, but it has "infected" other radical groups with its ideology that depicts the "United States as Islam's greatest foe."...

Mr. Tenet said al-Qaeda is continuing to recruit pilots and to evade new security measures in Southeast Asia, the Middle East and Europe.

"Even catastrophic attacks on the scale of 9/11 remain within al-Qaeda's reach," he said. "Make no mistake, these plots are hatched abroad, but they target U.S. soil and those of our allies."...

—*WASHINGTON TIMES*

C. Muslims Reassessing Their Schools After September 11 (6/7/02)

The burgeoning Muslim school movement in the U.S. is facing new challenges about its teachings and curriculum, especially concerning negative portrayals of America and non-Muslims, since September 11, reports the *Washington Post* (February 25). The growth of the Muslim population in the U.S. has generated a mushrooming of Islamic day schools....Reporters Valerie Strauss and Emily Wax write that the September 11 "attacks could serve as the catalyst in determining whether these schools and their students focus on the culture and politics of faraway Muslim lands or find within the Islamic tradition those ideas consistent with U.S. democracy and religious liberty."

To this end, some Muslim educators are writing new curricula that incorporate tenets of Islam with a "broadminded world-view." Textbooks from overseas that are often marked by their anti-American rhetoric are being replaced or re-edited. One school photocopies the pages needed for teaching while deleting those attacking Jews and Christians. The reporters note that these attitudes are also present among many teachers and administrators. On maps displayed in classes, Israel may be missing or crossed out, or teachers...will slip militant or anti-American comments into their lessons. Another concern is that some schools are funded by overseas groups, such as the Saudi government, that stipulate a militant Islamic curriculum.

Outside agencies, such as regional associations of schools and colleges, have not confronted Islamic schools on such issues.

—RELIGION WATCH

D. More Alleged Hamas Operatives and D.C.-Area Think Tank (10/8/04)

The Virginia man recently detained after his wife was seen video-taping Maryland's Chesapeake Bay Bridge has ties to a Springfield, Virginia Muslim think tank that is an alleged front for the terrorist organization Hamas. The think tank has been described as one of the "phony organizations that are really terrorist cells [and] part of the international terrorist network."

—CNSNews.com

II. Self-Proclaimed Goal of Making the U.S. a Muslim Country

A. American Islamic Lobby Goals Include Making U.S.A. a Muslim Nation (4/12/02)

[An] American Islamic advocacy group has planned a voter registration drive to coincide with the upcoming Muslim holiday at the end of the pilgrimage to Mecca.

The Council on American-Islamic Relations [CAIR], alleged to have ties to terrorist groups such as Hamas, says, "Our goal, if Allah wills, is to register more than 100,000 new Muslim voters over the next eight months."...

Observers of CAIR and similar organizations insist that, while these groups have a right to lobby just as any other public interest, their aims are suspect.

"They may not admit it, but ultimately they want to make the U.S. a Muslim country," Steven Emerson, a leading anti-terrorism specialist, told WorldNetDaily.

"In the interim they want to acquire as much political power as possible to push their agenda, to be afforded legitimacy by political officials," Emerson said. "So this...is part and parcel of their campaign."

CAIR spokesman Ibrahim Hooper indicated in a 1993 interview with the *Minneapolis Star Tribune* that he wants to see the United States become a Muslim country....

Abdulrahman Alamoudi, then-executive director of the American Muslim Council, said at a conference by the Islamic Association for Palestine in December 1996 that the United States will become a Muslim country, even if it takes 100 years....

CAIR Executive Director Nihad Awad said...that "recent events and new government policies have served to spur already growing political participation by American Muslims."...

Awad once worked for the Islamic Association of Palestine, considered by U.S. intelligence officials to be a front group for Hamas operating in the United States.

—worldnetdaily.com

B. They Are Seeking Acceptance for the Quran

1. Should Muslim Quran Be U.S.A.'s Top Authority? (7/4/03)

A former newspaper reporter says she stands by her story claiming the chairman of a leading Muslim lobby group declared the Quran should be America's highest authority.

In a press release accusing WorldNetDaily of "demonizing Muslims," the Washington, D.C.-based Council on American-Islamic Relations, or CAIR, denied its chairman of the board, Omar Ahmad, made the statement and said it is seeking a retraction from the newspaper that published the story July 4, 1998.

...Steve Waterhouse, editor of *The Argus* in Fremont, California,...told WND his paper has not been contacted by CAIR....

The reporter who covered the event, Lisa Gardiner, told WND she remembers the strong statement by Ahmad, who was one of several speakers at a session titled "How Should We as Muslims Live in America?" at an Islamic conference in Fremont.

Gardiner, regarded as a reliable reporter,...now a legislative aide,...said the statement in question is her paraphrase but insisted it is accurate and will not retract the story.

Her article also paraphrases Ahmad saying, "Islam isn't in America to be equal to any other faith but to become dominant."...

Ahmad's remarks have been cited by CAIR critics in the context of charges the group is tied to a radical element of Islam....

"CAIR's leadership," said [Joseph] Farah [WND editor], "has an Islamic totalitarian mind-set just like their funders in Saudi Arabia and their friends in the Hamas terrorist group. They dish it out pretty well, but they can't take any criticism....You should see the hate mail I get from CAIR's members. It would make your hair stand on end."

Farah added: "These extremists like to try to intimidate people, but they can't stand up like men and take it. Now they are running to the Justice Department for help. Fortunately for us, we don't have Shariah law in this country; we live free under the U.S. Constitution."

—WorldNetDaily

2. Muslims in America Now Pleading With Ecumenical Jargon (1/28/05)

"Behold! The angels said: 'O Mary! God giveth thee glad tidings of a Word from Him. His name will be Jesus Christ, the son of Mary, held in honor in this world and the Hereafter and in (the company of) those nearest to God.'"

Before searching for this quote in the New Testament, you might first [check] a copy of the Quran, Islam's revealed text. The quote is from verse 45 of chapter 3 of the Quran.

What is little understood, particularly in this holiday season, is that Muslims love and revere Jesus as one of God's greatest messengers to mankind. Other verses in the Quran—which is regarded by Muslims as the direct word of God—state that Jesus was strengthened with the "Holy Spirit" (2:87) and is a "sign for the whole world" (21:91). His virgin birth was confirmed when Mary is quoted as asking, "How can I have a son when no man has ever touched me?" (3:47).

The Quran shows Jesus speaking from the cradle and, with God's permission, curing lepers and the blind (5:110)....

As forces of hate in this country and worldwide try to pull Muslims and Christians apart, we are in desperate need of a unifying force that can bridge the widening gap of interfaith misunderstanding and mistrust. That force could be the message of love, peace and forgiveness taught by Jesus and accepted by followers of both faiths....

EDITOR'S COMMENTS: Islam "salutes" a lot of people they consider "prophets" (including Jesus), but you are to be well-advised that the Jesus they salute is not the Jesus who is the divine Son of the Almighty (Jehovah) God and who is the one and only Saviour for mankind.

It is a trick they employ to deceive. They are neither in sympathy with nor tolerant of Christians in any nation where they get the upper hand. Just look at Saudi Arabia and other Islamically dominated states to get a real view of how intolerant and inhumane they are when they have control.

This ecumenical style of appeal now going forward is a spurious appeal and should not be given one ounce of credibility by anyone.

3. CAIR Asks North Carolina Judges to Allow Use of Qur'an in Oaths (8/26/05)

A prominent national Islamic civil rights and advocacy group [has] called on judges...in North Carolina to allow use of the Qur'an, Islam's revealed text, when administering oaths.

The Washington-based Council on American-Islamic Relations (CAIR) said the current exclusive use of the Bible may be an inappropriate state endorsement of religion.

CAIR issued its call after Guilford County judges said they would not allow use of the Qur'ans in their courtrooms. "An oath on the Qur'an is not a lawful oath under our law," said W. Douglas Albright, Guilford's senior resident superior court judge. State law only refers to swearing an oath by putting a hand on the "Holy Scriptures." Those who do not wish to take an oath using the Bible may instead make an "affirmation."

A preliminary opinion...by North Carolina's Administrative Office of the Courts said that state law allows people to be sworn in using a Qur'an rather than a Bible.

4. Islamic Eschatology Draws on Christianity, Other Religions (7/15/05)

Christians will be surprised to learn that some of the end-times predictions in the Koran are very similar—even identical—to those in the Bible, according to a professor of Islamic studies at

Southwestern Baptist Theological Seminary.

Samuel Shahid, who has served on the faculty of the Fort Worth, Texas seminary since 1998, is the author of a new book, *The Last Trumpet: A Comparative Study in Christianity-Islamic Eschatology*, from Xulon Press.

Shahid writes, for example, that the Koran describes the end of time coming "suddenly and like the twinkling of an eye." It also says that only Allah "has the knowledge of the hour." Also, passages in the Koran teach that "a trumpet will blast on that day." These Koranic statements about the end times should sound familiar to Christians, Shahid said.

The similarities between the Koran's eschatological language and that of the Bible "are very striking," Shahid said. But that doesn't imply that the God of the Bible revealed the statements in the Koran to Muhammad.

"There is no doubt that they are not revealed; they are borrowed," Shahid said of specific eschatological statements in the Koran.

Even though he suspected that Islamic eschatology might be influenced by Christian eschatology prior to his comparative study, Shahid said his research revealed that Islamic eschatology also was influenced by Judaism, Zoroastrianism, apocalyptic materials, apocryphal materials and even Christian legends.

"When we talk about Islamic paradise and we compare it with the Zoroastrian paradise, you will be amazed to see the similarities between the two," he said.

Shahid, who was born and raised in Lebanon, has spent his academic career studying, teaching and writing about the beliefs, culture, history and literature of that area of the world.

—*BAPTIST PRESS*

C. Using the Political Process for Gains

1. Muslim Americans Say They Will Flex Political Muscle in 2004 (5/21/04)

New York (AP)—Nizar Yaghi hasn't decided for whom he'll vote on Election Day, but one thing is certain—the Muslim American will cast his ballot this November.

"After September 11, I understood that Muslim Americans need to come out and present themselves to the Americans," said Yaghi, a 28-year-old engineer from Schenectady, N.Y. "One way to do this is through the political process."

With the 2004 presidential election approaching, people like Yaghi are stepping up efforts to encourage their fellow Muslims to register to vote and to convince the presidential candidates that they need to be accountable to the Muslim American community, which numbers up to 7 million, according to estimates.

...Muslim groups say...they believe these voters could have considerable influence on the November election.

—cair-net.org

2. Muslim Vote Is Shifting to Democrats (4/9/04)

Across the nation, Muslims are about to send a very strong message through the ballot box to President Bush: We want change.

Although in years past most Muslims have typically voted Republican—identifying with the party's opposition to abortion and gay rights issues—this year the tide is expected to turn.

In a concerted effort, Muslim organizations...have started voter registration drives and are encouraging Muslims to vote Democrat....

Due to cultural influences and the fact many Muslims are immigrants, voting among Islamic communities has been fairly sparse....

But time has changed that. Many have become U.S. citizens, and new generations of American-born Muslims may make themselves a political force to be reckoned with in the future.

It's no secret that the pull of the effort originates from Bush's war on terrorism after 9/11.

—Council of American-Islamic Relations press release, 2/9/04

D. Campaign Through Public Relations Groups

1. American Muslims Promoting Their Image and Ideology (12/5/03)

The Council of American Islamic Relations announces daily their progress in getting their materials into public libraries across the U.S.A. Their October 15, 2003, press release states that already a sizeable package of books and tapes has been contributed to 6,942 public libraries.

With approximately 16,000 such facilities in the country, they are nearing the halfway mark.

Their concerns are to (1) polish up their tarnished image and (2) promote their Muslim ideology with the American people!

—Sword Press

2. The New Islam Remains the Same Old Islam By Paul M. Weyrich (3/28/03)

The Council on American-Islamic Relations, the American Muslim Council and other members of the American Muslim disinformation lobby are using generous donations from foreign lands to package a sanitized version of Islam as a peaceful and tolerant religion. But their fantasy Islam collides with the truth about life inside those countries where the religion is dominant. Unfortunately, too many Americans are willing to believe that Islam is a gentle lamb of a religion rather than the lion with blood on its claws, ready to pounce once more on unsuspecting innocents—and that it is being prodded to do so by its most devout believers. This does not mean that all Muslims are that way. But all it takes is a small minority who take its scriptures literally to destroy the peace of the nation and the world at large.

—CNSNews.com

3. U.S. Muslim Effort to Clear Stereotypes on Islam (12/3/04)

Seeking to create a better understanding between Muslims and non-Muslims in American society, Muslim activists have launched a mosque effort to assuage doubts and fears stemming from misconceptions about Islam.

On Tuesday, November 9, Florida's much-hit PalmBeachPost.com quoted Mohammad Osman Chowdhury, president of the Muslim Community of Palm Beach County, as saying, "Since September 11, people have been getting the wrong impression of Muslim people.

"We want to show others who we are. We are Americans, and we have a voice." Arena Maleque, 15, a Muslim student at Suncoast High School, said,..."People didn't understand the difference between ordinary Muslims and the terrorists. It took a while for them to understand that I'm a normal teenager. My religion is just different."...

The Muslim heartfelt effort includes inviting non-Muslims to share Iftar banquets with Muslims during the holy fasting month of Ramadan with around 300 people attending the event in a suburban West Palm Beach mosque....

The Southern California office of the Council on American-Islamic Relations—the largest U.S. Islamic civil liberties group—has also run radio advertisements intended to educate the public about Ramadan.

—cair-net.org

EDITOR'S COMMENTS: Islam's adherents in the U.S.A. are working hard to gain acceptance and to create a favorable opinion of their religion. Notice that they cleverly employ the statement of a fifteen-year-old high-school girl to pull on the emotions of the American people.

4. American Muslims Promoting Their Religion (12/17/04)

Earlier [in 2004] CAIR launched a nationwide television and radio public service announcement (PSA) campaign, called "I Am an American Muslim," designed to help reduce anti-Muslim discrimination and stereotyping.

Since then, almost 3 million people have viewed the 30- and 60-second PSAs and have offered positive feedback, one of which is the following:

"I just saw your marvelous 'I Am an American Muslim' public service announcement at 1:45 p.m., Saturday, November 13, on channel 25, South Bend, Indiana. Congratulations on producing such a marvelous, uplifting, positive image of American Muslims."

—cair-net.org

EDITOR'S COMMENTS: The "selling" of Islam to the American people is being spearheaded by a full-scale public relations and media blitz. It is propaganda which tells what they want to tell but does not begin to tell their real story.

5. U.S. Muslim Group to Offer Free Qur'ans (7/29/05)

On...May 17, the Council of American-Islamic Relations (CAIR) [held] a news conference at the nation's capital to launch a campaign to offer free Qurans to the American public. The campaign by the Washington-based Islamic civil rights and advocacy group is in response to a recent controversy generated by a *Newsweek* article alleging that Islam's holy text was flushed down a toilet.

CAIR's campaign, called "Explore the Quran," involves the community-sponsored distribution of Islam's revealed text to Americans nationwide.

...[S]aid CAIR executive director Nihad Awad, "It is our belief that greater access to Islam's holy book will help foster a better appreciation and understanding of Islam by ordinary Americans."

—cair-net.org

EDITOR'S COMMENTS: The Islam advocacy groups are pressing hard to legitimize themselves to the Western world.

E. Interim Goal of Mainstream Acceptance

1. America's Civil Religion (4/23/04)

A front group for a Hamas terrorist group wants to see the U.S. a Muslim country. Its spokesman said, "Islam is not in America to be equal to any other religion but to be dominant." Christianity's goal is for everlasting life. But Islam's goal is not the salvation of souls but the establishment of Koranic law in society. Ancient Rome was religiously inclusive, working all its cultural religions into a single civil religion. But its tolerance ended when it came to Christianity, which condemned the other gods as idols and insisted Christ is the only way to salvation. Religiously diverse America is becoming polytheistic (e.g., 9/11 "worship" service), [reflecting] a new civil religion with all "faiths" working together.

—*CALVARY CONTENDER*

2. Judeo-Christian Nation Challenged by American Muslims (8/1/03)

Muslim activists and organizations are pressing for greater Islamic inclusion in a society symbolized by the Judeo-Christian model. National Muslim groups, such as the American Muslim Council, the Council on American-Islamic Relations and the Muslim American Society, are trying to popularize such terms and concepts as "Judeo-Christian-Islamic" or "Abrahamic" (referring to Abraham) to include Islam as an American religion on par with Christianity and Judaism. "The new language should be used in all venues where we normally talk about Judeo-Christian values, starting with the media, academia, statements by politicians and comments made in churches, synagogues and other places," says Agha Saeed of the American Muslim Alliance, a political group headquartered in Fremont, California.

Aside from Muslim groups, such ecumenical organizations as the National Council of Churches have also joined the fledgling movement to drop or change "Judeo-Christian." The change is necessary and of symbolic importance for Muslims trying to find their role in the U.S. after September 11 and the Iraq war, according to proponents.

—RELIGION WATCH

EDITOR'S COMMENTS: The Muslims in the U.S.A. have initiated a "full-court press" to remake their image and to convince the American culture of their legitimacy! Folks, be wary and beware! Just look at the Middle East (almost any country) to get a sneak preview of what life will be like IF these people get a foothold here.

III. Their Allegiance Is to Islam, Not America

A. Arab-American Newspaper Shows Its Hand (9/13/02)

The Arabic-language "national weekly Arab-American newspaper" *Al-Watan,* published in Washington, D.C., San Francisco, Los Angeles and New York, has just featured two poems—"Yes, I Am a Terrorist," which extols the virtues of mass murderers, and "The Ape," which portrays President George W. Bush as a gorilla.

Al-Watan's stated mission is to provide Arab and Muslim Americans "with the most current, valuable, reliable and informative news on political, economic, social, cultural and educational issues, which concern the Arab-American community in their relations with the U.S. society at large."

—worldnetdaily.com

B. Muslim-Related Company Fires Woman for Eating Pork (8/27/04)

A Central Florida woman was fired from her job after eating "unclean" meat and violating a reported company policy that pork and pork products are not permissible on company premises, according to Local 6 News.

Lina Morales was hired as an administrative assistant at Rising Star, a Central Florida telecommunications company with strong Muslim ties, Local 6 News reported....

Morales, who is Catholic, was warned about eating pizza with meat the Muslim faith considered "unclean," Local 6 News reported. She was then fired for eating a bacon, lettuce and tomato sandwich, according to the report.

"Are you telling me they fired you because you had something with ham on it?" Local 6 News reporter Mike Holfeld asked.

"Yes," Morales said.

Holfeld asked, "A pizza and a BLT sandwich?"

"Yes," Morales said.

Local 6 News obtained the termination letter that states she was fired for refusing to comply with company policy that pork and pork products are not permissible on company premises....

The Koran forbids Muslims from eating pork. And according to Kujaatele Kweli [CEO of Rising Star], Morales and every employee at the company is advised of the no pork policy.

—local6.com

C. Muslim Unity Cited in Grenade Attack (7/18/03)

A U.S. soldier accused in a deadly grenade attack on his comrades in Kuwait said he did it because he believed American troops were going to rape and kill Muslims, an investigator testified [June 17] at Fort Knox, Kentucky. Sgt. David Maier spoke at a hearing to determine whether Sgt. Hasan Akbar, a Muslim, should face court-martial.

Akbar, 32, is accused of killing two officers and wounding 14 in the March 23 attack.

—*USA TODAY*

Chapter Nine
The Climate in the U.S.

I. Islam Seems to Be Making Advances Here

A. Mosques Outgrowing Churches in America (3/15/02)

New mosques sprang up in America more quickly than churches in the last decade, according to a new report. The number...grew by 42 percent between 1990 and 2000, compared with the 12-percent average increase for...churches, say researchers....

Professor David A. Roozen, director of the Hartford Institute for Religion Research, said that the immigration of professional Muslims in the last decade had been an important factor. "There are now many affluent Muslims in America—individuals with organizational skills and with sufficient financial means to build the mosques and Islamic centers that are now common all across our nation."

—CNS

B. U.S. Students Drawn to "Pure" Islam Studies (4/12/02)

Abdullah (the new Muslim name of a New Jersey youth) studies Islam at the Damaj Institute, the same school that John Walker Lindh, the so-called "American Taliban," may have attended, according to the local governor. It was here, as reported by the *Yemen Times* newspaper, that the then-teenager got his "fire." An MSNBC reporter visited two religious schools for boys (known as madrassas) in the towns of Tareem and Sa'dah, and found U.S. students at both.

The Damaj Institute, made up of classic mud structures in Sa'dah, focuses on the basic tenets of Islam. They dress and groom differently from other schools, with beards longer than normal, and are generally stern and less welcoming. Abdullah said he chose this school because it taught the purest Islam—the way it was interpreted in the time of Mohammed.

—RELIGION TODAY

C. Prisons Spawning Grounds for Militant Islam? (6/7/02)

Are U.S. and European prisons becoming prime recruiting grounds for militant Islam and even terrorism? In a report on Richard Reid, the suspected "shoe bomber" terrorist, in *Time* magazine (February 25), it is noted that like many others, Reid was converted to militant Islam while in prison. The magazine reports that since the early 1980s, "Bangladeshi and Pakistani imams, often associated with evangelist Islamic groups, have targeted young black inmates of British prisons." The literature brought by imams into the jails ranged from the Koran to pamphlets highlighting the importance of jihad. The *Minnesota Christian Chronicle* (January 24) cites a report in the *British Guardian,* finding that moderate Islamic clergy tend to be pushed aside by radical Muslims in British prisons.

...The Islamic Supreme Council, a small moderate Sufi-based organization, complains that their literature has been removed from American prison libraries by radical imams who claim it is "un-Islamic."

—RELIGION WATCH

D. Is the Islamic Call to Prayer a Liberty Issue? (6/4/04)

McMinnville, Ore. (BP)—Imagine you are nestled comfortably in your bed. It is officially morning but still dark outside. Suddenly a loudspeaker blaring an announcement accompanied by music invades your peace. The audible intrusion continues for almost two minutes. Now imagine this scenario occurring 365 days a year. The aforementioned is soon to be reality in the community of Hamtramck, Michigan.

The city council of the Detroit suburb voted unanimously April 20 to allow the Bangladeshi Al-Islah mosque to broadcast a call to prayer to its Muslim members via loudspeaker. The announcement will take place five times a day. Mosque leaders have agreed to refrain from airing the call before 6:00 a.m. and after 10:00 p.m.

Some said the call to prayer is the equivalent of church bells. Opponents argued that church bells have no religious significance. Both sides missed the point. Anything broadcast for two minutes over a loudspeaker before 9:00 a.m. is intrusive, regardless of content....

Many communities have noise ordinances restricting not only decibel levels but also the time of day when loud activity can be conducted. If Hamtramck does not yet have such an ordinance, I wonder how long it will be before it does. And will such a law be viewed as an infringement on the mosque's right to practice its religion?

Beyond the noise issue, I do have to take issue with the argument that the Muslim call to prayer is the same as church bells. Followers of Islam are expected to pray five times a day while facing Mecca. The call to prayer is a signal for members of a mosque to call on Allah.

The call to prayer is recited in Arabic. According to Ergun and Emir Caner, authors of *Unveiling Islam,* the call is as follows:

"God is great.
"God is great.
"God is great.
"God is great.
"I testify that there is none worthy of worship except God.
"I testify that there is none worthy of worship except God.
"I testify that Muhammad is the messenger of God.
"I testify that Muhammad is the messenger of God.
"Come to prayer!
"Come to prayer!
"Come to success!
"Come to success!
"God is great!
"God is great!
"There is none worthy of worship except God."

Most church bells indicate the time. Some play a portion of a hymn unaccompanied by lyrics. I have yet to encounter a church that broadcasts anything close to a message like the Muslim call to prayer.

If a Christian church wants to begin broadcasting a statement of faith five times a day, will the Hamtramck city council approve? What if a Baptist church wants to air a verse of Scripture like John 17:3, which states, "This is life eternal, that they might know thee the only true God, and Jesus Christ, whom thou hast sent"? Will it be accommodated?

While prayer five times a day is required of Muslims, I have found nowhere that a public call is mandated....

It is my understanding that there are other communities with significant Muslim populations that also allow the call to prayer to be broadcast. The American Civil Liberties Union and Americans United for Separation of Church and State seem to be missing in action on "the call to prayer" issue. Usually when there is a situation that even hints at a state accommodation of Christianity, the two groups are Johnny-on-the-spot to insist the public display or practice be stopped.

If the public display of the Ten Commandments, the mentioning of Jesus' name in a student-initiated prayer, and the recitation of "under God" in the pledge are viewed by "civil liberties" groups as an establishment of religion, then why is a Muslim call to prayer broadcast five times a day, 365 days a year, over a loudspeaker not viewed in the same light?

Can you say "hypocrisy"? Say it louder. Say it five times a day. Say it over a loudspeaker at 6:30 in the morning; the ACLU and AUSCS don't seem to be able to hear.

—Kelly Boggs

EDITOR'S COMMENTS: So when do they allow Christians to put up loud-speakers in the bell tower of the church and start making impassioned pleas that can be heard for blocks?

Folks, the politicians are blindly and naively caving in to the public-relations campaign of Islam. They use the Constitution against us and then use it for them! Come on!

E. CAIR-OH Educates Law Enforcement Agencies (6/18/04)

Columbus, Ohio—The Ohio office of the Council on American-Islamic Relations (CAIR-OH) held a joint educational seminar on April 20 with the U.S. Department of Justice Community Relations Service (CRS), the Columbus Community Relations Commission and the Ohio Civil Rights Commission (OCRC). The seminar, designed to foster cooperation between the Ohio Muslim community and law enforcement agencies, was attended by more than 60 central Ohio law enforcement officials.

"We were extremely pleased with both the large turnout and the great interest demonstrated by the officials in what CAIR had to say," said Jad Humeidan, executive director of CAIR-OH.

Representatives from the FBI, the Transportation Security Administration, the Columbus Police Department, the Westerville Police Department and the Franklin County Sheriff's Office attended the event.

Dr. Asma Mobin-Uddin, a pediatrician and vice president of CAIR-OH, led the discussion of Muslim beliefs and cultural practices....

"We would like to help law enforcement officials and Muslims have an appreciation for each other's needs and concerns," said Dr. Mobin-Uddin....

There are an estimated 150,000 Muslims in Ohio. CAIR, America's largest Islamic civil liberties group, is headquartered in Washington, D.C., and has 26 regional offices and chapters nationwide and in Canada.

—cair-net.org

EDITOR'S COMMENTS: Wake up, wake up, wake up! The Islamic public relations machine is quietly setting up a "fifth column" inside our country!

F. Islamic Beliefs Enter Mainstream (9/10/04)

When the Islamic call to prayer was allowed to be broadcast through the streets of Hamtramck, it thrust religious tradition into the national spotlight and illustrated the growing influence of Muslims in the multiethnic enclave.

But the religious and cultural practices of Muslims in Metro Detroit are taking hold on a much quieter and broader scale with schools, businesses, hospitals, funeral homes and even cemeteries adjusting to meet their needs.

At Henry Ford and St. John hospitals, policies have been adopted that allow Muslim women to maintain their religious modesty during medical treatment. East-facing graves are being added at cemeteries like White Chapel in Troy to meet the growing demand for graves facing Mecca. And schools in Hamtramck and Dearborn are tailoring schedules and offering halal food that meets the dietary needs of Muslims.

...Sally Howell, a University of Michigan graduate student and member of a research team that studied Metro Detroit Arabs last year, [said,] "Mainstreaming their culture is a boost to them, but perhaps more important to the rest of the community to increase our understanding of them."

—Doug Guthrie, *DETROIT NEWS*

G. American Muslims "Train" FBI Agents on Islam and Muslims (12/31/04)

The Florida office of the Council of American-Islamic Relations (CAIR-FL) today held a diversity training workshop on Islam and the American Muslim community at the FBI's Jacksonville Division All Employee Conference.

More than 150 law enforcement agents, including FBI and Joint Terrorism Task Force supervisory personnel, attended the workshop that examined basic Islamic beliefs and concepts, common stereotypes of Islam and Muslims and ways in which to improve interactions with the Muslim community....

CAIR-FL hopes that it will continue to expand the program to help train law enforcement authorities in other parts of the state, just as it did...in Jacksonville and earlier in Miami.

—cair-net.org

II. Liberal Elements Support Acceptance of Islam

A. In the Public and Private Sectors

1. Officials Complain About Islam Textbooks (8/30/02)

Still smarting from a federal court order that made them remove postings of the Ten Commandments from government buildings, Hamilton County officials complain that the federal government published textbooks promoting Islam.

"It's atrocious," Hamilton County Commissioner Harold Coker said about textbooks financed by the United States and sent to Afghanistan. Some of the textbooks for grades 1–12 include Islamic teachings and Koran verses.

Commissioners have seized on the textbooks, paid for by the U.S. Agency for International Development, as an example of government hypocrisy. The texts are being edited and printed at the University of Nebraska for $65 million.

"That's taxpayers' money that paid for those books," County Commissioner Ben Miller said. "The Ten Commandments plaques we used were purchased with private money and donated to the county."

The textbooks were printed in response to an urgent request from Afghanistan officials trying to rebuild the country after U.S. troops helped drive the Islamic fundamentalist Taliban regime from power, AID spokeswoman Kathryn Stratos said.

—*NASHVILLE TENNESSEAN*

2. State Hires Anti-American Muslim Prison Chaplains (11/21/03)

A New York senator has called for an immediate investigation of all 42 Muslim clerics working for the State Department of Correctional Services. State Senator Michael F. Nozzolio (R.-Seneca Falls), chairman of the Senate Crime Victims, Crime and Correctional Committee, said the arrest on federal charges of Osameh Al Wahaidy of Fayetteville, N.Y., a Muslim chaplain at the Auburn Correctional Facility, is an embarrassment. Al Wahaidy, a Jordanian working in the United States, has been charged with helping to send aid to Iraq through a charity in violation of U.N. sanctions. Until recently, the state prison system relied almost exclusively on one person to recruit its clerics, Warith Deen Umar, who has been linked to anti-American propaganda. The correction department barred him from New York's prisons after the *Wall Street Journal* quoted him as saying the September 11 hijackers should be honored as martyrs. Two other Muslim clerics, or imams, in the New York state prison system have been accused of anti-American activity since September 11.

—*PULPIT HELPS*

3. Ohio's Council on American Islamic Relations Receives ACLU Liberty's Flame Award (12/19/03)

COLUMBUS, Ohio—The Ohio Chapter of the Council on American-Islamic Relations (CAIR-Ohio) has been selected to receive the American Civil Liberties Union of Ohio's (ACLU-Ohio) annual Liberty's Flame Award for contributions to the advancement and protection of civil liberties.

The award [was] presented at a program and reception on Saturday, October 25, in Columbus, Ohio....

CAIR-Ohio and the ACLU of Ohio have been working together on projects defending the constitutional rights of Muslims.

There are an estimated 150,000 Muslims in Ohio, 7 million in the United States, and 1.2 billion worldwide.

CAIR, America's largest Islamic civil liberties group, is head-quartered in Washington, D.C., and has 16 offices nationwide and in Canada.

—From the CAIR press

EDITOR'S COMMENTS: Does the ACLU have a penchant for the absurd and ridiculous, or what?

4. Hallmark Cards for Muslim Holy Day (1/2/04)

[In 2003], Hallmark unveiled its newest "holiday" card, for Eid al-Fitr, which sold out quickly....

Eid al-Fitr, the end of the Muslim holy month of Ramadan, was celebrated November 25....

—*NASHVILLE TENNESSEAN*

5. South Carolina Scouts Serving Allah and America??? (9/10/04)

Under an American flag, after a plaintive rendition of the "Star-Spangled Banner," almost 300 scouts received khaki scout hats and merit badge armbands Sunday....

The York County Sheriff and the head of South Carolina's FBI office clapped and handed out certificates.

Then the campers recited the Koran and pledged their lives to Allah.

Sunday's award ceremony was for the Muslim Scouts of America after a month-long camp held at Islamville, a 40-acre tract outside York....

Muslims of America stresses Islam while affirming patriotic values and commitment to America....

...The FBI's Les Wiser, special agent in charge of South Carolina, told the camp graduates that America celebrates its differences and unity at the same time. The camp's ideals of trustworthiness, loyalty and service are the same values as he learned in scouts decades ago.

"My duty is to protect diversity," Wiser told the campers and their families. "I'm here to build trust between you and me."...

"Brotherhood," said Nasir Abduul-Wadud of Springfield, Massachusetts. "Unity. Leadership. We learned so much here."

—heraldonline.com

EDITOR'S COMMENTS: Out of the ashes of September 11, Islam is rising

to prominence inside the country. The well-orchestrated effort to "sell" Islam to the American people is a slick public relations maneuver. We continue to say that Islam is the avowed enemy of Christianity and, we believe, of America as well.

6. Film About Muhammad to Open in Theaters Nationwide (11/5/04)

The release of *Muhammad: The Last Prophet* is scheduled to coincide with Eid ul-Fitr, the holiday marking the end of the Islamic fast of Ramadan. The 90-minute film, produced by the creators of animated classics such as *The King and I* and *The Fox and the Hound* for Badr International, will be shown in theaters in 37 U.S. and Canadian cities for one week beginning November 14.

—cair-net.org

EDITOR'S COMMENTS: The coddling of Islam and its promotion in America are epidemic! Beware!

7. Ramsey Clark to Defend Saddam; Former Attorney General Says Hussein Victim of "Selective Prosecution" (2/25/05)

Ramsey Clark, former U.S. attorney general [Lyndon Johnson administration] and leftist antiwar activist, announced [December 29, 2004] he has joined the defense team of former Iraqi president Saddam Hussein.

Clark made the announcement in Amman, Jordan, and took the opportunity to slam the Bush administration, saying the U.S. should be tried for alleged "war crimes" in...Iraq....

...Clark visited Hussein in Baghdad in February 2003 just before the U.S.-led invasion [Agence France-Presse]. He first met the dictator prior to the first Gulf War. The news service reports Clark has also been involved with the defense of former Yugoslav leader Slobodan Milosevic, on trial for war crimes in The Hague....

Referring to the former despot as "President Saddam Hussein," Clark says it's the U.S. that should go on trial, pointing to last [November's] siege of Falluja, destruction of houses, alleged torture in prisons and the military's role in the deaths of thousands of Iraqis.

—worldnetdaily.com

EDITOR'S COMMENTS: When you see this on the television news, you should know that Ramsey Clark, though a former U.S. attorney general,

is a radical leftist who now runs the International Action Center, a front group for the communist Workers' World Party. He is a frequent and longtime critic of much that is American.

B. In Education

1. Parents Sue School Over Muslim Orientation (8/30/02)

(CNSNews.com)—A public school in Byron, California is being sued after forcing Christian students to pretend they were Muslims for three weeks. As part of an Islam simulation project, students prayed in the name of Allah, chose a Muslim name and played a "jihad" dice game, according to the Michigan-based Thomas More Law Center, the group that filed the lawsuit. "What's at issue is the true meaning of the Establishment Clause," said Richard Thompson, the law center's chief counsel.

2. Fourth Graders to "Celebrate" the Dead (SWORD Editor Learns Kids Being Taught Islam Too) (12/20/02)

Fourth graders at McNear Elementary in Petaluma City, California will be celebrating the dead in a week-long classroom ritual designed to simulate the Mexican holiday "El Dia de los Muertos," or Day of the Dead.

In a letter sent to parents by the public school teachers,...the traditional Meso-American holiday will be observed from October 28 to November 1 as an alternative to the celebration of Halloween where youngsters traditionally wear costumes and hold classroom parties....

The ancient Aztec El Dia de los Muertos ritual celebrated in Mexico and in Mexican communities throughout the United States typically involves honoring the dead by donning wooden skull masks and dancing on the graves of deceased relatives or at altars built in their honor. The altars are surrounded with flowers, food and pictures of the deceased. Celebrants light candles and place them next to the altar....

The Aztecs and other Meso-American civilizations believed the deceased come back to visit during the ritual. As the flier sent to Petaluma City parents describes, El Dia de los Muertos is a "ritual event in which the spirits of dead loved ones are invited to visit the living as honored guests."...

The United States Justice Foundation…objects to the event on the grounds that the school's sponsorship amounts to an endorsement of a particular religious view….

The foundation states the materials distributed to parents and teachers describing the event "are replete with references to 'altars,' 'ritual,' 'ofrenda,' 'symbolic items,' 'cycle of life,' 'remembrance,' 'dead animals,' welcoming 'death' and other clearly religious themes" and "clearly indicate that the entire event is intended to be a 'celebration' and practical application of these spiritual and religious themes."…

McNear principal Clare Eckhardt denies the event is unconstitutional and maintains the school is merely following state guidelines for curriculum.

…Eckhardt told WorldNetDaily, "We're required to describe the social, political, cultural and economic life and interactions among the people of California from pre-Columbian societies to Meso-American societies. As you know, California has a significant Latino population, and this helps build an understanding between the two major cultural groups in our community."

—worldnetdaily.com

EDITOR'S COMMENTS: When I preached November 3 in southern California, I mentioned publicly my recent book, *Islam: A Raging Storm*. After the service, several junior-high-age young people came to my book table and said, "We're learning about that in our public school." When I inquired of them for details, I was told that their hour-long social studies class was being devoted to "informing" them about Islam! The double standard is obvious, deliberate and blatant!

3. NYC School Bars Nativity Scenes, Allows Menorahs and Islamic Crescents (12/5/03)

In a dispute over display of holiday symbols, New York City schools are allowing Jewish menorahs and Islamic crescents but barring Christian nativity scenes, alleging the depiction of the birth of Christ does not represent a historical event.

In pleadings with a federal court in defense of the ban, New York City lawyers asserted the "suggestion that a crèche is a historically accurate representation of an event with secular significance is wholly disingenuous."

The Jewish and Islamic symbols are allowed, the district says, because they have a secular dimension, but the Christian symbols are "purely religious."

Robert J. Muise, who [challenged] the school policy at a federal court hearing...in Brooklyn, told WorldNetDaily he believes most Americans don't see it that way.

"The birth of Jesus is a historical event which serves as the basis for celebration of Christmas," Muise stated. "It's of importance for both Christians and non-Christians."

Muise's Michigan-based Thomas More Law Center filed a motion to temporarily restrain the city from enforcing its ban on nativity scenes. The center asserts New York's policy "promotes the Jewish and Islamic faiths while conveying the impermissible message of dis-approval of Christianity in violation of the U.S. Constitution."

The Michigan group says one public-school principal issued a memo encouraging teachers to bring to school "religious symbols" that represent the Islamic and Jewish religions, but made no mention of Christianity.

—WorldNetDaily

4. Okay to Keep Teaching Islam in California School (4/23/04)

A federal judge has ruled that a California school district may con-tinue requiring seventh-grade students to make believe they are Muslims, wear Islamic garments, memorize Quran verses, etc. The [plaintiff's] chief counsel said: "While public schools prohibit Christian students from reading the Bible, praying, displaying the Ten Commandments, and even mentioning the word 'God,' students in California are being indoctrinated into the religion of Islam."

—*CALVARY CONTENDER*

5. Atlantic City Schools to Recognize Islamic Holidays (7/2/04)

Atlantic City, N.J. (AP) —Atlantic City has become the fourth school district in New Jersey to recognize Muslim holidays.

The city's board of education approved districtwide days off for Eid al-Fitr and Eid al-Adha, two sacred Islamic holidays, for the upcoming school year.

Previously, under state law Muslim students and teachers were allowed to take off Islamic holidays without being penalized. According to Superintendent Fredrick P. Nickles, about 560 of the city's 7,800 children are Muslim.

Board member Cornell Davis, who is Muslim, called the decision "courageous."...

"It shows a lot of character about us as Americans," Davis told *The Press of Atlantic City*....

To fit the two holidays into the school calendar, officials reduced the number of days schools can take off for emergencies from six to four....

School districts in Trenton, Paterson and Irvington already recognize Islamic holidays.

EDITOR'S COMMENTS: Political correctness, which is the pandering mind-set of the liberal theorists, seems to have a dual agenda. They attack everything Christian and accommodate anything else!

6. Free Speech Double Standard on California Campus (4/8/05)

A Kuwaiti Arab Muslim student is speaking out after his community college approved an article indirectly comparing him to Adolph Hitler. Last semester, Foothill College political science professor Joseph Woolcock flunked Ahmad Al Qloushi and ordered him to get psychological treatment because he wrote a pro-American essay as his take-home final exam. Standing his ground on the essay, Al Qloushi explained that if it were not for U.S. intervention into Kuwait when he was younger, he would not have had the opportunity for furthering his education. Woolcock filed a school grievance against Al Qloushi, charging him with intimidation and harassment for mentioning his name to the media. Now comes word that the Foothill College Student Activities Office has approved an article that labels Al Qloushi "irrational" and accuses him of endangering Woolcock. The seventeen-year-old freshman says he cannot understand why the school would allow a "terrible personal attack" on him. "I just don't understand why they would approve something which personally attacks me and compares me to one of the most evil dictators on the face of the earth," the student says. Al Qloushi happens to be chairman of the campus group Foothill College Republicans. Administrators have told that group it is not allowed to include the school's name in a press release regarding its chairman.

—*RELIGION TODAY*

EDITOR'S COMMENTS: I saw this young man on a TV interview. He is bright, articulate and very pro-American in his views. As a result, his professor ordered him into psychotherapy under the threat of the revocation of his visa. It is another compelling case of the intolerance of liberals when they are in control. It also echoes the fact that liberals do hold sway on university campuses almost everywhere.

C. In Religion

1. Baptist Liberals (CBF) Voice Support for Muslims (8/30/02)

ATLANTA (BP)—The executive director of the Cooperative Baptist Fellowship has issued a statement "to express publicly a very different perspective on Muslim-Christian relationship than the one conveyed recently at the Southern Baptist Convention," according to the CBF's Internet news page.

Daniel Vestal...issued the statement June 20 in response to remarks by Jerry Vines...in St. Louis June 10. Vines referred to Muhammad as a "demon-possessed pedophile" and claimed that the religion of Islam breeds terrorism....

Vestal's statement read:

"As a Baptist Christian who formerly was affiliated with the Southern Baptist Convention, I wish to convey my deepest sorrow and regret over recent statements made by Southern Baptist leaders. This rhetoric is not in the Spirit of Christ, and it negatively affects the mission of the church in the world.

"To malign or denigrate the historic or current leaders of Islam contradicts our Christian commitment of love for all people. We desire the highest good for all Muslims and grieve with you over the pain such remarks have caused. Please be assured of our respect and our desire for true friendship as well as open, courteous, sincere dialogue."...

Judy Battles,...the fellowship's coordinator in Texas, was quoted in the *Fort Worth Star-Telegram* June 24 as saying..., "I think Dan [Vestal] spoke out to let people know that there are different kinds of Baptists. We don't need to condemn Muslims."

EDITOR'S COMMENTS: The liberal mind-set is so out of kilter that no matter how extreme a situation is, they just can't seem to get off on the right side! The Cooperative Baptist Fellowship, an offshoot from the Southern Baptist Convention, is a haven for liberals!

2. Methodists Set Up "Dialogue" With Muslims (11/22/02)

(AgapePress)—United Methodists and the Muslim community will be entering a four-year national dialogue next year....Anne Marshall, a spokesperson for the Commission, says that two major Muslim groups have praised the United Methodists for initiating attempts at "interfaith understanding." However, not everyone thinks the ecumenical give-and-take between the two religious groups is a good idea. Mark Tooley, executive director of United Methodist Action, says this is a continuation of the overall trend in mainline churches to give priority to dialogue with leaders of false religions, thereby de-emphasizing evangelism and the message of Christ. "The way in which the dialogue is waged, that ultimately is the sad result, is that the Gospel is compromised, the uniqueness of Jesus Christ is compromised," he says. "And I'm afraid...it ends up giving the appearance of...saying that all religions are, in essence, equally true." Members of the United Methodist Commission on Christian Unity and Interreligious Concerns say through the dialogue they hope to explore what they call "a deeper understanding of Islam."

—RELIGION TODAY

EDITOR'S COMMENTS: If these liberal ideologues are so naive as to feel such a study necessary, we recommend they extract their heads from the sand just long enough to review the news for the past fifteen months! Even a casual look around should render their projected four-year dialogue both unwise and unnecessary.

3. Liberal Church Leaders Do Not Represent People in the Pews on Iraq War (5/9/03)

FAIRFAX, Va.—According to leaders of the Association of Church Renewal (ACR), church statements opposing war with Iraq do not represent the views of most members of those churches. The ACR is an ecumenical association of mainline church organizations committed to advocating orthodox Christian teaching and practice in their respective denominations.

"This is not a new phenomenon," said James Heidinger of *Good News,* a magazine dedicated to renewal in the United Methodist Church....

A recent Gallup poll confirmed this observation, noting that opinion among Christians about possible war with Iraq tracks closely with national opinion. In fact, 60% of those who found religion to be "very important" in their lives supported military action against Iraq....

Parker Williamson, editor of the *Presbyterian Layman,* said, "The simple fact is that in this issue...ecclesiastical bureaucrats are making statements that most of their members would disavow...."

Heidinger had strong words for the National Council of Churches (NCC), which has sent antiwar delegations to France, Germany, Italy, Russia and Great Britain. A spokesperson for the NCC delegation to France said his group represented "the official position of the National Council of Churches, with 50 million members in 36 denominations, and the Roman Catholic Church, with nearly 64 million U.S. members," implying that they spoke for over 110 million American churchgoers.

"It's ludicrous for the NCC to claim such a thing," Heidinger said. "It is simply untrue. American Christians, while certainly not eager for war, are still largely in support of the president's policy."

Williamson commented that this was a particularly egregious example of misrepresentation by the NCC. "The NCC claim is false....Lying to the people of France, Germany, Italy, Russia and Britain about the opinion of Christians in the United States misleads the European public...."

—ACR [Association for Church Renewal] news release

EDITOR'S COMMENTS: Reports March 24 on a poll conducted by the *Washington Post* and NBC and reported on the networks showed support for the war at 75 percent. This is not the first indication that the liberal NCC crowd is "out to lunch" on their theology and common sense as well.

4. Churches Vow Humanitarian Aid to Focus on Food, Not Conversion (5/23/03)

Mainstream religious groups from the United States, including the Southern Baptist Convention and the United Methodist Church, are prepared to send envoys into Iraq to distribute humanitarian aid once the all-clear has been given.

The aid will include food, water and other necessities, and that's all—no New Testaments or religious tracts on the side, the groups say.

"The purpose in going is to demonstrate how much God loves people and to simply demonstrate in a physical way the love of God," said Mark Kelly, spokesman for the International Mission Board of the Southern Baptist Convention....

But the Council on American-Islamic Relations, with headquarters in Washington, D.C.,...isn't so sure....

"All I can say is that I hope the people of Iraq don't know what they have been saying about Islam...," said Rashid Naim of the council's Atlanta office....

"...Otherwise, their security cannot be guaranteed, I think."
—*NASHVILLE TENNESSEAN*

EDITOR'S COMMENTS: What is said and what isn't said here are both revealing! The fact is, Islam and its adherents are intolerant of the views of anyone else.

These groups with their well-intentioned relief efforts are saying up front that no literature will be sent! Then the representative from CAIR says if the Iraqi Muslims know about the comments made by some of the Christian leaders about Islam, it could compromise the safety of the relief workers! The liberation of Iraq does not yet mean that the people will be free to choose their faith. That is another war yet to be fought.

5. Charismatics Use the Quran to Preach Jesus Among Muslims (3/11/05)

Many Christians denounce the Quran's teachings, but some believers have taken the controversial approach of using Islam's holy book to bring Muslims to Jesus. They say by communicating the gospel in a manner Islamists can understand, many receive Christ. Their converts are called "Messianic Muslims," partly because they are encouraged not to abandon some Islamic traditions.

"I use their own book of precepts to validate the authenticity of Christ," said Patricia Bailey, who has ministered in many Arabic nations. "If Muslims embrace the Quran as their holy book, then it is the ultimate tool to reach them and at least to provoke them to question what is written in their own book of the law. The Quran makes references to the Bible. The Bible never refers to the Quran for truth or authenticity."...

Bailey is not alone in her provocative way of reaching Muslims. John Taimoor is an itinerant preacher...[of] a California-based ministry that presents Christianity within an Islamic context....

A Messianic Muslim is an Islamist who has accepted Jesus but refuses to be referred to as a Christian and chooses to stay within the Arab community....

"In fact, at every cardinal point of the Gospel, it contradicts the Word of God," said Don McCurry, president of Colorado-based Ministries to Muslims, who served for eighteen years in Pakistan as a missionary.

McCurry...said he has "a big problem" with the name Messianic Muslims. "In the dictionary, 'Muslim' simply means someone who is submitted," he said. "Muslims will tell you that it means someone submitted to God. But the bottom line is that 'Muslim,' in a Muslim's eyes, means someone submitted to Muhammad and his version of God."

[David] Goldmann [missions consultant] concurred, noting that "a Christian who calls himself a Messianic Muslim will only confuse people."

"The biblical approach is for a Christian to associate himself with Jesus Christ of Christianity," he said....

Taimoor admitted that some Christians do not understand his strategy. "If some do accuse me of compromise or heresy, it is because they do not understand the linguistic and cultural significance, or they expect the Gospel to be westernized before it is preached," he said.

—CHARISMA

EDITOR'S COMMENTS: Here is another case of "method doesn't matter," doing anything to get to preach Christ. It appears that this time both method and message have been significantly compromised.

As much as we need to get the Gospel to the Muslim world and as important as it is for them to be saved, we must never contaminate the process in our zeal to do it.

Although some charismatics have spoken against the practice, it is another unfortunate development in the ecumenical arena.

When biblical views, biblical standards, biblical prohibitions and biblical guidelines are viewed as "doctrinal" and optional, then these unwise, heretical practices are sure to come.

The problem here is not westernization; it is whether or not compromise to the point of heresy is justified. We say, "No!"

III. There Are Some Who Have Not Been Fooled

A. National Commentators Have Courage to Tell Truth

1. Muslims Ask Dr. Laura to Apologize for "Tirade" (1/16/04)

WASHINGTON—A prominent national Islamic civil rights organization [November 19] called on nationally syndicated radio talk show host Dr. Laura Schlessinger to apologize for what the group called an "anti-

Muslim tirade" on her November 17 program. ("Dr. Laura's" radio program is heard by 12 million listeners on some 270 stations nationwide.)

The Washington-based Council on American-Islamic Relations (CAIR) said it received a number of complaints from Muslims who said Schlessinger's remarks crossed the line from legitimate commentary on terrorism to Islamophobic bigotry.

The offensive comments came in response to a mother who asked whether her 16-year-old daughter should take part in a Catholic high-school class field trip to a local mosque. The purpose of the field trip was to have the students in a "moral themes" class learn how "Muslims are treated" in America.

Schlessinger said in her response: "This is a class on morals. What is the point of going to a mosque?...You're joking, of course....How many Americans have tortured and murdered Muslims?...I think you ought to stand up against this class and this teacher. This is despicable. You tell him you are willing to go to the mosque only if it is one that has done its best to rout out terrorists in its midst...instead of complaining....I am horrified that you would let her go....I am so sick and tired of all the Arab-American groups whining and complaining about some kind of treatment....What culture and what religion were all the murderers of 9/11?...They murdered us....That's the culture you want your daughter to learn about?"...

In 2002, CAIR sent a letter to Schlessinger asking for a clarification of her on-air claim that there is a "Muslim plan" to take over the world.

—Islam Infonet

EDITOR'S COMMENTS: The lady behind the microphone is right on this one. The goal of world domination religiously and governmentally by Muslims is such an obvious and well-documented reality, it would appear childish to debate it.

2. Paul Harvey Says Islam "Encourages Killing" (1/30/04)

WASHINGTON—The Council on American-Islamic Relations (CAIR) is calling for an on-air apology from syndicated radio commentator Paul Harvey, who said on his [December 4] program that Islam "encourages killing."

Harvey, who has 24 million weekly listeners on some 1,600 radio stations in this country and around the world, made that claim during his [December 4] commentary.

In that segment, Harvey described the bloody nature of cockfight gambling in Iraq and said: "Add to the thirst for blood a religion that encourages killing, and it is entirely understandable if Americans came to this bloody party unprepared."...

In 1999, Harvey issued an on-air apology to Muslims for remarks suggesting that Islam was a "fraudulent religion." The apology came after hundreds of concerned Muslims called, faxed and e-mailed both Harvey's office and that of ABC Radio Networks, his program's syndicator.

—Islam Infonet

EDITOR'S COMMENTS: The facts are the facts! Denials and apologies cannot cover up the long history of Islam's violence and its daily atrocities now being perpetrated all over the world.

B. Many Americans Are Thinking for Themselves

1. New Poll Reflects American Mind-Set (6/21/02)

Americans have mixed feelings about religion and violence after September 11, a new survey reports.

What's more, while Americans are more trusting of Muslims in the United States, they continue to worry about anti-American sentiments in Islamic countries worldwide, said the poll released on March 20 by the Pew Forum on Religion and Public Life.

On the role of religion, 80 percent of Americans rank it as beneficial....

The report found that 67 percent of respondents said that the United States is a "Christian nation." But more Americans—75 percent—also said that "many religions can lead to eternal life," not just Christianity.

Despite this support of religious pluralism, the concern over violence focused on Islam.

—*WASHINGTON TIMES*

EDITOR'S COMMENTS: The wishy-washy views of the American mind in the twenty-first century are disturbing. Such a mind-set makes clear that the doctrinal truths of the Bible are not in vogue with most people. It also reflects the urgency with which we all should respond. Help us get the SWORD into the hands of people everywhere. It is one proven method of making a difference and getting results!

2. Church's "Anti-Islam" Sign Causes Flap (10/10/03)

An Indiana minister defended his decision to place his sermon topic, "Islam: America's Number One Enemy," on his church sign

[September 7]. Marc Monte, pastor of Faith Baptist Church of Avon, located near Indianapolis, said the message he preached the Sunday before the two-year anniversary of the September 11 terrorist attacks was meant to provide needed information for the public, the *Indianapolis Star* reported.

"I [wanted] to stir interest, not alarm, but Islam is a false religion, dangerous and hate promoting," said Monte, who has pastored the 350-member congregation for more than five years. "If I were a pastor who read KKK literature or Hitler's *Mein Kampf,* I would hope the members of my church would head to other churches. It is awful stuff. I repudiate it, and I put Islam in the same camp."

But some area residents viewed the sign as hate speech more than a needed warning. "To call Islam an 'enemy' seems to be a message of hate," said Susan Jones, who passed the marquee twice a day [September 1–7]. "It is just arrogant and ignorant, and I can't get past it. It is disheartening that a pastor, a pillar of the community, would be preaching this."

—CNS

EDITOR'S COMMENTS: Brother Monte is a good man who is doing a good job in this Indianapolis suburb. His stand on the Islam issue needs to be repeated by thousands of local church pastors across the land. The politicians will rarely do right on any issue of controversy until the pulpits cry loudly with the needed message!

3. Knowledge of Islam Increases Negative Opinions (10/10/03)

NASHVILLE, Tenn. (BP)—An increase in the percentage of Americans who believe Islam encourages violence stems from an upsurge in knowledge about the religion itself, a seminary professor who converted from Islam to Christianity says.

A poll by the Pew Research Center for the People & the Press found that a plurality of Americans—44 percent—believe that Islam is more likely than other religions "to encourage violence among its believers." The finding, released July 24, is a sharp increase from the 25 percent who answered the same way in March 2002....

Emir Caner, a professor at Southeastern [SBC]...Seminary, Wake Forest, North Carolina, attributes the changing numbers to Americans' learning more about the teachings and history of Islam.

"[So] many people are now studying Islam," said Caner, an assistant....Those same people "have come across disturbing passages within the Koran that, if taken literally," mean that Islam is "militant in its purest form."

"They [also] see in its history, from its outset, that physical force has been used from the time of Muhammad until basically the colonial period of American and British empires."

4. Christians Puzzled Over Bush's "Same God" Remark (1/16/04)

Many...Christians in the U.S. say they are outraged over President George Bush's statement that Christians and Muslims worship the same God.

The statement was made [November 20] during the joint press conference in England with Prime Minister Tony Blair. A reporter noted Bush has frequently expressed the view that freedom is a gift from "the Almighty" but questioned whether Bush believes "Muslims worship the same Almighty" as the president and other Christians do.

"I do say that freedom is the Almighty's gift to every person. I also condition it by saying freedom is not America's gift to the world," Bush replied. "It's much greater than that, of course. And I believe we worship the same god," reported the *London Telegraph*....

Blair avoided answering the same question, replying with a general statement about freedom.

Bush, a practicing Christian who frequently talks publicly about the importance to him of his faith, nevertheless, has repeatedly defended Islam as a religion of peace, ever since the September 11, 2001, terror attack on the U.S. by 19 Islamist radicals....

Gary Bauer, former presidential candidate and president of American Values, [said] Bush's comment is "not helpful to the president. Since everybody agrees he's not a theologian, he would be much better advised to punt when he gets that kind of question."

—WorldNetDaily

EDITOR'S COMMENTS: In our view, the issue is not whether he is theologically savvy or not. We believe the president is well-advised and knows exactly what the truth is.

It appears that he has chosen, for reasons related to politics and international diplomacy, to make these conciliatory statements. Whatever his reasons for doing so, we know that the man-made god known as Allah is NOT the great God Almighty who created the universe. Maybe the president doesn't feel he can say so; we do not feel so inclined to be silent!

C. Even Some Muslims Are Opening Their Eyes

1. Cleric Deceptively Decries Violence in Name of Islam (4/8/05)

Saudi Arabia's top cleric told 2 million pilgrims from around the world...Islam's greatest problems are that its own sons are being "lured by the devil" into militancy and a hostile world is conspiring against it.

The pilgrims converged on Mount Arafat for the climax of the hajj; their eyes welled with tears as they prayed on the most critical day of the annual pilgrimage the faithful believe will wipe away their sins.

Sheik Abdul-Aziz al-Sheik, speaking at a mosque near Mount Arafat on the climactic day, lamented the violence waged by Islamic militants against Saudi Arabia.

"The greatest affliction to strike the nation of Islam came from some of its own sons, who were lured by the devil. They have called the nation infidel, they have shed protected blood, and they have spread vice on earth with explosions and destruction and killing of innocents."...

Men and women, otherwise not allowed to mix in the conservative kingdom, rubbed shoulders and stretched helping hands to [one another] as they climbed the uneven but gentle slope. Many already atop pushed and shoved to hug a pillar, standing where Islam's seventh-century prophet Muhammad gave his last sermon in the year 632, three months before his death.

—NASHVILLE TENNESSEAN

EDITOR'S COMMENTS: Take careful note! The "hostile world" he mentions would be the U.S.A. and Israel, as well as all Christians and Jews.

This cleric laments specifically "protected blood" and "killing of innocents." In the Muslim world both terms are understood as referring to the killing of Muslims. Naiveté in the western world assumes he's trying to be a voice of reason to discourage the violence everywhere! Not at all! This carefully worded disavowal of violence is about Muslims killing Muslims. Unfortunately, the cleric did not include the rest of us in his concerns.

2. Bin Laden Support Waning in Muslim Nations (9/9/05)

Osama bin Laden's standing has dropped significantly in some key Muslim countries, while support for suicide bombings and other acts of violence has "declined dramatically," according to a new survey released.

...Andrew Kohut, president of the Pew Research Center, an independent think tank in Washington, and director of the project, [said,] "U.S. and Western ideas about democracy have been globalized and are in the Muslim world."

—*NASHVILLE TENNESSEAN*

EDITOR'S COMMENTS: Getting a view of democracy and life outside the Islam tyranny states will indeed change their minds. That was a major factor in the fall of the USSR, and we can expect it will also get some results among the Muslims. But let's not be lulled to sleep by such encouraging polls. There are millions of these Islamists who are committed to our demise.

For a complete list of books available from the Sword of the Lord, write to Sword of the Lord Publishers, P. O. Box 1099, Murfreesboro, Tennessee 37133.

(800) 251-4100
(615) 893-6700
FAX (615) 848-6943
www.swordofthelord.com